CONTEMPORARY'S

THE WRITE STUFF

Putting It in Paragraphs

Lois B. Jones and
Jane L. Evanson

UPDATED EDITION

Field-Test Coordinator
Joyce A. Duffy
Austin Career Education Center
Chicago, Illinois

Update Editor
Erica Pochis

Editorial Director
Caren Van Slyke

CB

CONTEMPORARY BOOKS

a division of NTC/CONTEMPORARY PUBLISHING COMPANY
Lincolnwood, Illinois USA

Library of Congress Cataloging-in-Publication Data

Jones, Lois B.
    Putting it in paragraphs / Lois B. Jones and Jane L. Evanson.
        p.   cm. — (Contemporary's the write stuff)
    ISBN 0-8092-3836-5 (paper)
    1. English language—Paragraphs.   2. English language—Rhetoric.
I. Evanson, Jane L.   II. Title.   III. Series.
PE1439.J66   1992
808'.042—dc20

92-20429
CIP

ISBN: 0-8092-3836-5

Published by Contemporary Books,
a division of NTC/Contemporary Publishing Company,
4255 West Touhy Avenue,
Lincolnwood (Chicago), Illinois 60646-1975 U.S.A.

8 9 0 QB(D) 16 15 14 13 12 11 10

Editorial	Art and Illustrations
Cathy Niemet	Princess Louise El
Ellen Frechette	Ophelia M. Chambliss-Jones
Karin Evans	
Christine M. Benton	Typography
Sarah Schmidt	Terrence Alan Stone
Claudia Allen	
Ilene Weismehl	Design
Katherine Willhoite	Deborah Rank Popely
Leah Mayes	
	Cover Design
Production Editor	Georgene Sainati
Patricia Reid	

Front cover photo © Kelly Harriger, WestLight

Inset photo by C. C. Cain Photography

Table of Contents

NOTES TO THE INSTRUCTOR..iv

CHAPTER 1: GETTING READY TO WRITE...**1**
Why Write?   *1*
The Process of Writing   *1*
How Should I Get Ready?   *2*
Answers   *12*

CHAPTER 2: WRITING A TOPIC SENTENCE..**14**
What Is a Paragraph?   *14*
What Is a Topic Sentence?   *19*
Sentence Highlight #1   *23*
What Is the Relationship of the Topic Sentence to the Paragraph?   *29*
Chapter Checklist   *33*
Answers   *34*

CHAPTER 3: WRITING A WHOLE PARAGRAPH......................................**38**
Unity and the Topic Sentence   *38*
Unity and Supporting Sentences   *41*
Organizing Your Ideas   *48*
Sentence Highlight #2   *56*
Chapter Checklist   *61*
Portfolio Activity #1   *63*
Answers   *65*

CHAPTER 4: PARAGRAPHS: TELLING AND DESCRIBING......................**69**
The Purposes of Paragraphs   *69*
Writing a Narrative Paragraph   *76*
Sentence Highlight #3   *78*
Writing a Descriptive Paragraph   *80*
Sentence Highlight #4   *86*
Sentence Highlight #5   *88*
Chapter Checklist   *89*
Portfolio Activity #2   *91*
Answers   *92*

CHAPTER 5: PARAGRAPHS: PERSUADING AND INFORMING...................**97**
Writing a Persuasive Paragraph   *97*
Sentence Highlight #6   *105*
Writing an Informative Paragraph   *107*
Sentence Highlight #7   *112*
Chapter Checklist   *113*
Portfolio Activity #3   *114*
Answers   *115*

CHAPTER 6: EDITING YOUR WORK...**119**
What Is Editing?   *119*
Is Your Punctuation Correct?   *120*
Is Your Capitalization Correct?   *122*
Did You Check Your Spelling?   *124*
Do You Have Any Run-on Sentences?   *125*
Are All Your Sentences Complete?   *125*
Portfolio Activity #4   *128*
Answers   *129*

CHAPTER 7: USING MODELS...**132**
How to Use This Chapter   *132*
Personal Writing   *132*
Business Writing   *136*
Portfolio Activity #5   *139*

Notes to the Instructor

Many students are reluctant to write because they are afraid of making mistakes in grammar and spelling. They are also unsure of what to write about. They worry that everything they put onto paper is final and must be perfect. These concerns prevent many people from ever getting started writing.

Your students need to know that almost everything they read has been changed and rewritten several times before they even see it. They need to look at **writing as a step-by-step process**. The first and most important step is getting their thoughts down on paper. Following the steps in the process will simply help make their writing more understandable for the reader.

Putting It in Paragraphs will guide your students through the writing process with a step-by-step approach. As much as possible, the student should concentrate on one step at a time. Let students know that **there will be plenty of time later to fix up their work**. This book provides grammar hints along the way, called *Sentence Highlights*, and students should be encouraged to use this help in their work. This book also contains **five portfolio activities** in which students evaluate their own paragraphs in order to learn more about the writing process and their writing abilities.

The purpose of this book is to help students write **well-organized, well-reasoned paragraphs**. Starting carefully with the development of topic sentences and supporting ideas, this book helps students write **narrative, descriptive, persuasive, and informative paragraphs**. Most important, students are introduced to a rich variety of writing experiences ranging from self-expression to the practical needs of everyday life.

It is a good idea to do the prewriting and writing exercises along with your students. In this way, you can demonstrate that even experienced writers learn by writing. Encourage students to share their writing with other students. Since writing is really an attempt to inform the reader, an informal exchange of papers will help the writer get a better idea of how to improve his or her work.

By the time your students finish this book, they will have developed both proficiency as writers and, more important, confidence in their writing ability.

1. Getting Ready to Write

Why Write?

People write because they have something they want to say. The writing process begins long before you start using a pen and paper. It begins when you start thinking about what you want to say. It may be as simple as a message you need to leave for a roommate or family member. You think about it for a few seconds, organize your thoughts, take a piece of paper, and write:

> "I'll be home at six o'clock. Please put the casserole in the oven at five-thirty."

In other cases, what you want to write may be as formal as a business report about what you have accomplished during the past year. You'd need to think more than a few seconds about what you want to say, and you probably would want to organize your thoughts on paper before you start the report.

In either case, there is nothing to fear. In both of these situations, you know better than anyone else what you want to say. If you were asked to describe your job or school accomplishments out loud, you would have little trouble doing so. Instead, you must use *writing* to express yourself. What you want to say does not change, but how you say it does.

The Process of Writing

The most important thing to realize right now is that **writing is a step-by-step process**. Just as you take several different steps to solve a difficult math problem, you also need to take separate steps to write a sentence, a paragraph, or an essay. Remember that putting something on paper does not mean that it has to be permanent. You may change your mind while writing, and this is fine. Most writing that you see has been changed and rewritten several times before you read it.

What About Grammar?

What you write comes from inside of you—your thoughts, feelings, opinions, memories, and observations. You need to put these ideas on paper without worrying about how they will look at first. Grammar and spelling are important, but not as important as taking the first step of putting something on paper. Once you have written something, you can go back and fix whatever grammar or spelling errors you may have made. If you worry too much about mistakes as you write, you will never get to say what you want.

You will see that the editing (correcting) chapter is toward the end of this book. This is because editing is the last step in the writing process. It is an important step, but no more important than getting your ideas across. As you work through Chapter 1, you'll notice that you will not be asked to write a complete sentence. Why? The reason is that you are on the first step of the writing process. You are *getting ready to write*. In later steps you will be writing sentences and paragraphs.

How Should I Get Ready?

In this book, you will first have a chance to *get ready to write*. The prewriting activities will help you start thinking about what you are going to say when you do write. First, choose a time and a place that are good for you. Some people have a quiet hideaway and write after things have settled down for the night. Others find that they need a more formal spot such as a desk at school, the library, or the office. Think about what would be best for you. You should also consider sharing your writing with a friend—perhaps someone who is also doing some writing. By reading and discussing each other's work, you will learn even more about what makes good writing and what does not.

Many writers find it helpful to keep a file of their work. You too will do this so that you can see how much your writing has improved.

Finally, keep writing. The more you write, and the more comfortable you become with your own writing, the more it will improve. You may also find that writing will help you to organize your thoughts, and you may begin to better understand your own ideas and feelings.

Before You Begin Writing

Many people say that getting started is the hardest part of the whole writing process. These three questions should help you get going:

1. What is my topic?
2. Why am I writing about this topic?
3. Whom am I writing for?

Let's look at these three questions one at a time.

STEP 1. WHAT IS MY TOPIC? If you have chosen or been assigned a topic in class or on a test, this question is easy to answer. A topic can be anything from "my commute to work today" to "rent control in public housing." If you are choosing a topic for yourself, choose one that interests you and that you know something about.

Whether your topic was assigned or chosen by you, write it down. Even if you think you know what your topic is, writing it down helps make it clear in your mind.

If your piece of writing is not an assignment or a test, you'll have to think a little more about what your topic is. Don't assume you have decided on a topic and start writing right away. You may realize later that you really don't have a clear idea of what your topic is. For example, if you are writing a letter of complaint, what is your topic? Is your topic a space heater that does not work? a moldy loaf of bread you just purchased? poorly lit streets in your neighborhood? Once you decide this, write it down.

STEP 2. WHY AM I WRITING ABOUT THIS TOPIC? People write for many reasons. If you know your purpose before you start, you will be able to present your ideas more clearly. One purpose for writing is *to inform*. To inform means to share information or to give knowledge without opinion, as in a newspaper report. You are informing when you list facts that give specific answers to questions such as *who, what, when, how,* and *why.* You are informing when you list changes made in safety procedures at your plant or when you tell a friend how your plan to start your own business works.

Another purpose for writing is *to persuade,* or to convince, someone why things should or should not be. When writing for this purpose, you will be expressing your values, opinions, and preferences. You will be trying to convince your reader to accept them. For example, when you write a memo telling your supervisor why you deserve a raise, you are writing a *persuasive* piece. An advertisement for a product is also an example of *persuasive* writing.

A third purpose in writing is *to describe* a person, place, object, or situation. To describe means to give a picture in writing. The reader should be able to visualize whatever is being described. You are writing a *descriptive* piece when you tell a friend how to recognize your sister when she gets off the train. You are also being descriptive when you tell how George and Antonio look when they have their childish arguments over who has to finish a job.

The last purpose for writing is *to tell a story.* Telling a story is reporting what happened. You could report a short incident, such as a funny scene you saw in a movie, or tell a longer story about the six days you spent in a hospital. This kind of writing is called *narrative.*

Almost any topic can be developed to fulfill any of the four purposes. For example, as you look out your front window, you see a tall spruce tree that you could *describe*—tell what the tree looks like. You could *inform*—explain the tree's different parts and how they work. Or you could *tell a story*—tell where and when you got the tree, how fast it grew, and how you decorate it over the holiday season. Finally, you could *persuade*—convince the reader that the tree should not be cut down when the city widens the road.

Therefore, just knowing your topic does not mean you have already decided on your purpose. Look at the topic you have written down and ask yourself why you are writing about it. Do you want to tell a story about it? give your opinion on it? give someone information about it? or describe it?

The chart below sums up the four writing purposes and what they are used for.

INFORMATIVE	**PERSUASIVE**
1. give directions 2. explain "how to" do something 3. answer questions *who, what, when, how, where* 4. make something easier to understand	1. convince reader of something 2. sell ideas or products 3. take a side on an issue 4. state an opinion
DESCRIPTIVE	**NARRATIVE**
1. create a picture 2. help reader "see" details 3. give characteristics	1. tell what happened 2. give a history of something 3. narrate an account of an event

Exercise A: Knowing Your Purpose

For each item below, the purpose is identified. Circle the letter of the topic that would best suit this purpose. Use the chart on page 4 to help you.

EXAMPLE: DESCRIBE
a. why Jay deserves a promotion
b. the condition of your home after the flood
c. how to repair a broken waterline

1. INFORM
   a. my opinion on abortion
   b. the new suit you bought for a job interview
   c. how to fill out a 1040 tax form

2. TELL A STORY
   a. what happened to Tom at the sales convention
   b. how to carve a turkey
   c. who will be transferred to the production department

3. DESCRIBE
   a. how to decide if fruit is ripe
   b. how a handgun works
   c. what the new delivery van looks like

4. PERSUADE
   a. how to pitch a tent
   b. a popular country-western song
   c. why the budget for your department should be increased

5. INFORM
   a. what happened when your wallet was stolen
   b. what your son looked like when you gave him a bicycle
   c. directions for catching trout

6. PERSUADE
   a. the new safety regulations at school
   b. why you should change your vote
   c. where the new hospital will be built

7. DESCRIBE
   a. the look on Sharon's face when she was fired
   b. what information to include on a résumé
   c. why Mr. Gutierrez retired

8. TELL A STORY
   a. events leading up to Derek's drug addiction
   b. the date of the next group meeting
   c. the beauty of the Grand Canyon

ANSWERS AND EXPLANATIONS ARE ON PAGE 12.

Exercise B: More About Purpose

Below you will find different situations described. Try to put yourself in each particular situation and imagine what your writing purpose would be: *to inform, to persuade, to describe,* or *to tell a story.* Then write down the reason you chose this as your purpose.

EXAMPLE: In a letter to a newspaper editor about increased crime in the community, the writer states:

> "Therefore, I feel we must demand that the City Council approve funding for more police officers and patrol cars. . . ."

PURPOSE: *to persuade*

The writer's purpose is to *convince someone that we need funding for police and patrol cars.*

1. In a letter to a friend about his trip to California, Lenny states:

   > "After I left the base in San Diego, I took the train directly to Los Angeles, where I took a tour of the MGM studios. What a terrific vacation this has been!"

   PURPOSE: _____

   The writer's purpose is to _____

   _____

2. In a letter to a family-counseling organization, a woman writes:

   > "Please help me put my life back in order. A member of my church told me that you have services for people like me. I want my children to live with me again, and I should try making things work with my husband. Is there someone there who can give me the help I need?"

   PURPOSE: _____

   The writer's purpose is to _____

   _____

3. In a student organization's magazine, one writer says:

> "Classes began today, and the well-kept school grounds were filled with hurrying students and talkative teachers. Desks were already beginning to overflow with papers and books. The usually silent library was a bustling scene of new energy, as men and women made plans for their upcoming classes."

PURPOSE: _____

The writer's purpose is to _____

_____

4. In an entry blank for a recipe contest, Larry writes:

> "First, remove ribs from refrigerator and let sit until at room temperature. Next, mix the marinade made up of soy sauce, ketchup, red wine vinegar, a dash of salt, two tablespoons of lemon juice, and a teaspoon of thyme. Put ribs in a deep bowl and pour marinade over top. Let sit for two hours before baking."

PURPOSE: _____

The writer's purpose is to _____

_____

5. In a love letter to her boyfriend, Tamika writes:

> "The days are long and lonely without you. The sky is never blue, and the sun does not shine. My face is just a dreary sight, pale and gray with sorrow. The smile I used to wear has turned into a sour frown, and my eyes are damp with tears."

PURPOSE: _____

The writer's purpose is to _____

_____

6. A memo from the post office concerning new window hours states:

> "New hours will be from 9:00 A.M. to 5:30 P.M. Monday through Saturday. As usual, we are closed on Sundays."

PURPOSE: _____

The writer's purpose is to _____

_____

7. In a letter to his elderly mother, Juan writes:

> "I really think you would be better off having someone to take care of you during the day. I would certainly do it if I were able, but since this is impossible, perhaps we should consider a nursing home. Not all of them are as bad as you think—let's at least look at one or two."

PURPOSE: _____

The writer's purpose is to _____

_____

8. In a newspaper article about an armed robbery, the author writes:

> "Yesterday, two masked women entered a downtown bank at noon. They carried pistols and forced bank patrons to lie on the floor. Tellers were then ordered to put all money in a brown leather suitcase. When the money had been placed in the case, the two women escaped through a back door."

PURPOSE: _____

The writer's purpose is to _____

_____

POSSIBLE ANSWERS ARE ON PAGES 12 AND 13.

STEP 3. WHOM AM I WRITING FOR? You speak in different ways to different people. You use different tones of voice. You choose different words, facts, and details. This is also true of your writing. Before you begin to write, think about your reader. Will the reader be your teacher or boss, a co-worker, a friend, your spouse, a parent, a child, a neighbor, or a group of strangers? Recognizing your reader will not only influence what you write but how you write it. It will affect which words you use, what examples you give, and how simple or how complex your writing is.

Perhaps you've had an argument with a co-worker. It's going to be difficult to go back to work on Monday unless you settle things. You may discuss your problem one way with a casual acquaintance and another way with your spouse. You'd talk about it differently with your boss. So, you could easily explain the argument in three different ways.

1. To your spouse:
   "Leonard had better get his act together, or I won't work with him much longer."
2. To an aquaintance:
   "A co-worker of mine, Leonard, is really hard to work with. Something has to be done."
3. To your boss:
   "Leonard and I are having some difficulties working with each other. I think that we should sit down and discuss the situation."

Notice that in each situation the speaker chose words to suit the "audience." You will do the same when you write.

Now imagine that you had a car accident. You drove the company car from work, and you stopped to meet some friends on your way home. As you pulled out of the the parking lot, a truck hit you on the passenger side. No one was hurt, but the car had to be towed from the scene.

Think about what you would tell each of the following people about the accident: (1) your best friend or spouse, (2) the police officer, and (3) your boss. You would probably describe the accident differently to each one. You may include some of the same details, and you may leave some out, depending upon whom you are talking to. You also may put the details in a different order to emphasize certain points and not others. Read the accident descriptions below and see if you can figure out who the audience of each piece is.

Don't worry—nobody was hurt. I stopped as I always do at Joe's, and as I was leaving, some jerk hit me on the passenger side. What will Mr. Romero say about the car, though?

I was driving home from work, and I had to make a stop. As I pulled out of my parking space, a large green pickup truck came out of nowhere and hit me full speed. I'm sure it was the other driver's fault.

You aren't going to believe what happened. As I was driving home from work last night, somebody hit the front right side of the company car. The damage is not all that bad, and I'm sure it can be fixed in a short time. Let me assure you that insurance will cover the damages.

If you could see that in the first paragraph, the "audience" is a friend or spouse, in the second paragraph it is the police officer, and in the last one, the "audience" is the speaker's boss, you are on the right track. Notice that the first thing the speaker says to the close friend or spouse is that no one was hurt. The speaker does not mention the type of truck that hit the car, but does feel free to mention that friends were also in the car. The police officer hears something rather different. No mention is made of the friends, but the speaker emphasizes details about the other driver. In the last speech, the speaker emphasizes the condition of the car—a matter of importance to the speaker's boss.

When you write, you decide to say certain things in certain ways, depending on who your reader is. This is why it is important to answer the question "Whom am I writing for?" before you begin to write.

Remember that your reader does not have to be a specific person. Your reader might be a group of people whom you do not know at all. In this case, you'll have to decide whether you should be formal or informal with this group and whether this group knows anything about your topic.

Once you have decided who your main audience or reader is, jot it down somewhere. From time to time as you write, you can look back at this and keep your reader in mind.

Exercise C: Knowing Your Reader

Each of the paragraphs below is intended for a specific reader. Circle the reader you think each paragraph is written for. Look at all the choices carefully and find the *best* answer.

1. The video I saw last night was really great! It was called *The Birds* and was directed by Hitchcock. I can't believe how scared I was through the whole thing! There were birds flying everywhere, attacking everyone in sight. You have to see it.

   a. a group of movie critics   b. your work supervisor
   c. a friend or acquaintance   d. a small child

2. The movie called *The Birds*, directed by Alfred Hitchcock, is a frightening horror story. In the expertly filmed picture, a flock of birds invades a small town and destroys all people in its

path. Many of the scenes are violent, and the suspense built up by Mr. Hitchcock makes this an excellent, but frightening, movie.

    a. a close relative   b. your best friend

    c. a group of teenagers   d. a teacher

3. The workers in this plant feel that we have been unjustly treated by management. We believe that it is time to sit down and discuss our problems. Instead of seeing our conditions improve over the years, we find that things are getting worse. We need a management team that will listen to what we have to say.

    a. a casual acquaintance   b. the plant manager

    c. angry union members   d. your spouse

4. The workers in this plant are sick and tired of giving in to the demands of the big shots. The quality of our lives rests in their ungrateful hands, and we have had enough! Our needs are small compared to theirs, yet they cannot give an inch. They don't even listen!

    a. fellow union members   b. the plant manager

    c. the company lawyer   d. a casual acquaintance

5. Sue and I are at the end of our rope. If we don't get the check from the government we've been waiting for, our plans will be ruined. We had planned to use the extra cash for a little trip together. Sue and I have worked hard for a long time, and this check is a break we really deserve. I'll let you know how it turns out.

    a. a friend or relative   b. a social security officer

    c. someone the writer   d. a police officer
       doesn't know very well

6. My wife, Susan Parson, and I are writing to ask about the check owed to us by the government. As you know, we are senior citizens, and we count on this income to provide us with the bare necessities of life. Without this money, we are not sure we can survive. We hope you will please consider our situation and help us in this matter.

    a. a relative   b. a casual acquaintance

    c. a social security officer   d. a good friend

ANSWERS ARE ON PAGE 13.

ANSWERS

Exercise A

1. (c) This is the only choice that would call for giving information. Choice (a) asks for an opinion, which would be persuasive, and choice (b) would be a topic for a descriptive paragraph.

2. (a) A paragraph about what happened to Tom would tell a story. Choices (b) and (c) would give information.

3. (c) This topic describes what the van looks like. Choices (a) and (b) would give information.

4. (c) A paragraph about why the budget should be increased would give an opinion, or persuade. Choice (a) would inform, and choice (b) would describe a song.

5. (c) Directions for catching trout would make an informative paragraph. Choice (a) would tell a story, and choice (b) would describe the boy.

6. (b) A paragraph about why you should change your vote is an example of persuasive writing. Choices (a) and (c) would give information.

7. (a) You could certainly write a descriptive paragraph about how Sharon looked when she was fired. Choice (b) would simply give information, and choice (c) would either give information or tell a story.

8. (a) Events leading up to Derek's addiction would be in a paragraph that tells a story. Choice (b) would simply inform someone of the facts, and choice (c) would describe the Grand Canyon.

Exercise B

The purposes given here are the correct answers. Your information about what the writer's purpose is may be worded differently from what you see here. That's OK. These are meant to be models for you to compare your answers with. Don't worry if your ideas are slightly different from these.

1. **Purpose:** to tell a story

   The writer's purpose is to: tell what happened on his trip to California

2. **Purpose:** to persuade

   The writer's purpose is to: try to get help from a counselor for her family

3. **Purpose:** to describe

   The writer's purpose is to: tell what the first day of classes looked like

4. **Purpose:** to inform

   The writer's purpose is to: tell someone how to make ribs

5. **Purpose:** to describe

   The writer's purpose is to: describe her feelings about her boyfriend and to say how she feels when he is not around

6. **Purpose:** to inform

   The writer's purpose is to: inform customers about the new post office hours

7. **Purpose:** to persuade

   The writer's purpose is to: persuade his mother to consider moving into a nursing home

8. **Purpose:** to inform

   The writer's purpose is to: inform readers about what happened in a bank robbery

Exercise C

Remember that you should choose the *best* answer. It is possible that these paragraphs could be written to another of the choices, but you should try to see whom the writer really intended to write to.

1. (c)   The writer uses casual language, so he or she probably isn't writing to a group of movie critics or a work supervisor. Also, the writer probably would not be recommending such a scary movie to a small child.

2. (d)   This paragraph is written in a formal and nonfamiliar way, much like essays assigned by teachers. This formal style would probably not be used when writing to the other choices.

3. (b)   In a letter or memo to a plant manager, an employee would use this tone and word choice to discuss a problem. If the employee were writing to angry union members, the language would probably sound angrier and even more forceful. The writer would also not use this formal style with an acquaintance or a spouse.

4. (a)   This writing is more like what you might write to fellow union workers. The writer certainly would not use descriptions like "big shots" and "ungrateful hands" if he or she were addressing the manager or lawyer. Also, the writer probably wouldn't use this strong language if writing to a casual acquaintance.

5. (a)   This person writes casually, as if to a close friend or relative. The other choices would all call for a different approach and writing style.

6. (c)   This person is asking for help in a very formal manner. He needs to mention his wife's full name, so he surely can't be writing to a friend or relative. Choice (c) is the only logical answer.

2. Writing a Topic Sentence

What Is a Paragraph?

Most writing is either one paragraph or a series of paragraphs. A **paragraph** is a group of sentences that all develop a single topic or idea. We write in paragraphs because they help us to organize our ideas and make them clearer to the reader. You can tell when a new paragraph begins by the indent, or short space, before the first word.

Characteristics of a Paragraph

How do you write a paragraph? How can you be sure you are developing one main idea? It will help if you can see that a paragraph should have two important characteristics. First, you should write a **topic sentence** that states the main idea of what you want to say. Second, you should support or explain your idea. The sentences that follow your topic sentence are called **supporting sentences**. You should combine a topic sentence with carefully written supporting sentences to write a well-developed paragraph.

Here is an example of a paragraph that has these two important characteristics.

> *Everyone should save some money for "rainy days."* These rainy days come in the form of illness, losing a job, moving, or any other unexpected event. Since such circumstances can cost extra money, it is very important that you have some funds set aside to cope with emergencies. This type of planning will give you and your family greater peace of mind.

MODEL
Topic Sentence and Supporting Sentences

This model paragraph is well written. The main idea, that everyone should save some money for rainy days, is stated in the first sentence. The remaining sentences develop that idea. Sentence two tells what is meant by rainy days. Sentences three and four emphasize the importance of saving money.

Now look at the series of sentences below.

> Everyone should save money for "rainy days." Last month, my nephew lost his job and got sick. I am careful with my dollars, and I'm a good planner.

If sentences are not clearly related to a main idea, you have only a series of disconnected sentences, not a paragraph. All the sentences above are about "rainy days," but they do not express and support one main idea.

> **To summarize, a paragraph must have**
> - a main topic or idea
> - sentences that all relate to the main idea

Exercise A: Recognizing Paragraphs

Read each item below. Then put the letter "P" in the space before each item that is a paragraph and the letters "NP" before each item that is not a paragraph. To decide this, ask yourself (1) What is the main idea being expressed? and (2) Do all of the sentences relate to this idea?

_____ 1. Once our baby could sit up and crawl, she became interested in undoing everything she could. She tossed toys from her crib, pulled yarn out of a basket, and emptied purses. As her crawling improved, she emptied shelves, boxes, and drawers.

_____ 2. Doug was sure he had caught the biggest trout in the county. Many people enjoy eating fish. Fishing is Doug's favorite pastime. He spends a lot of time at a stream near his house. One trout he caught was over a foot and a half long.

_____ 3. People should be allowed to pay their home heating fuel bills in equal installments over the course of the year. Budgeting for $30 in one part of the year and then having to pay $75 in another is unfair and often impossible for the consumer. Oil companies have many more assets than the average consumer. They should pass on some of their huge profit to consumers by allowing them to pay heating bills in installments.

_____ 4. Ana Maria, as usual, was frustrated and irritated by Manolo's actions. She had fixed a nice dinner, and now Manolo was not going to get off work until eight o'clock. She wondered why he had not called her before six to let her know. Her plans for the whole evening were ruined.

_____ 5. To get the most out of your garden plot, it is necessary to plan ahead. Planning is a useful skill. The traditional shape for a garden is a rectangle. A rectangle is an easy shape to plow, but others might be more interesting. Planning your garden will help you avoid unnecessary uprooting and replanting.

_____ 6. Football is a sport seen by more American TV viewers than any other sport. TV is a wonderful invention that lets millions of armchair athletes feel the thrill of many different kinds of sports. TV also brings educational programs into many homes.

_____ 7. A car can be a human's best friend—that is, as long as it keeps running. Getting to work, going out on a date, taking the family on vacation, and going shopping are all reasons for having and enjoying a car. The car can be a faithful friend. But, when it decides to sputter and stop in the center lane of some busy expressway, the friendship can fall apart pretty fast.

_____ 8. The following steps are necessary to build a fire properly. First, make sure your wood is good and dry. Fireplaces are actually a poor source of heat because the draft draws warm air from the room. It is usually necessary to use some newspaper to get the fire going. If you are using a fireplace, make sure the flue is open.

ANSWERS AND EXPLANATIONS ARE ON PAGE 34.

The Structure of a Paragraph

Well-written paragraphs have a solid structure. Like a story, paragraphs have a beginning, a middle, and an end. The beginning is the **introduction**. It states the point or main idea of the paragraph. Most often, this is the **topic sentence**, which we will examine in more detail later in this chapter. The topic sentence, as mentioned before, tells the reader what the paragraph is going to be about.

The middle of a paragraph is called the **body**. This is the part of the paragraph that supports and develops the main idea that is stated in the topic sentence. It presents ideas that illustrate or explain the topic sentence. Many different kinds of supporting sentences can be used, depending on your topic and the main idea that you wish to discuss. Later, we will discuss how to decide exactly what supporting ideas to use in a particular paragraph. The important thing to understand now is that the sentences in the body of the paragraph must clearly support the topic sentence.

At the end of a paragraph there is sometimes a **closing** or **concluding sentence**. This is the part of the paragraph that summarizes or restates what has been presented. Sometimes the closing sentence leads the reader to an insight about the topic discussed in the paragraph. Sometimes, in a piece of writing that has more than one paragraph, the closing sentence of a paragraph leads into the paragraph that will follow.

Not every paragraph needs a closing sentence. Repeating the topic sentence idea or summarizing the details at the end of a short paragraph might be too much. While you want to be certain that your readers understand and remember your idea, you do not want to bore them by repeating yourself.

When you do need to sum up the contents of your paragraph, however, a good closing sentence repeats in different words the main idea expressed in your paragraph.

Below is an example of a well-structured paragraph. It has the three basic parts of a paragraph: **topic sentence**, **supporting details** or **body**, and **closing** or **concluding sentence**.

> *Keeping a pet may be beneficial to your health.* Research shows that stroking a pet eases tension and can lower blood pressure. Talking to your pet also releases tension, provides companionship, and sometimes leads your thoughts to the solution of a problem. Walking a pet can also provide regular exercise, which, of course, is a key to good health. Although pet ownership may not guarantee that you will live 105 years, some aspects of your health may improve.

MODEL
**Three Parts
of a
Paragraph**

Exercise B: Recognizing Paragraph Parts

The following groups of sentences are not in correct paragraph order. Put the letter "T" after the topic sentence, the letter "S" after the supporting sentences, and the letter "C" after the closing sentence.

1. a. In fact, I'd rather go back to the days when radio and books were our only sources of entertainment! ____
   b. Even some of the so-called "educational" shows are nothing more than mindless cartoons. ____
   c. Filled with blatant sex and brutal violence, prime-time hours are unfit for my younger children. ____
   d. The quality of television programs has really gone downhill. ____

2. a. Credit cards can be a wonderful blessing or a terrible curse. ____
   b. If used carefully, they can allow planned, deferred payments. ____
   c. When used carelessly, they bring almost hopeless debt and anxiety. ____
   d. Each cardholder is responsible for deciding whether these cards will be a good thing or a bad thing. ____

3. a. I am writing you because I would like a refund for the enclosed T-shirt I ordered from your company. ____
   b. But, as you can see, my size 10 has now become a size 2 after washing it just once. ____
   c. Please refund my $4.95 plus shipping as soon as possible. ____
   d. Your advertisement clearly stated that the shirt would not shrink. ____

4. a. There are so many makes and models to choose from. ____
   b. The options on each model are too numerous to count. ____
   c. Since there are so many decisions to make, the process can surely take a long time! ____
   d. Financing comes in about as many packages as candy does. ____
   e. The decision to buy a new car is one that takes a lot of thought. ____

5. a. Many people have very strong feelings about the issue. ____
   b. The government announced that its athletes will not come to the Olympics. ____
   c. Some are very glad and say good riddance. ____
   d. Most American athletes are disappointed by the decision. ____
   e. No matter how you look at it, the whole situation is unfortunate. ____

ANSWERS ARE ON PAGE 34.

What Is a Topic Sentence?

A topic sentence summarizes the main idea of a paragraph in one sentence. It is, therefore, the most important sentence in a paragraph. How can you tell if your topic sentence provides a clear and adequate introduction to your paragraph? Below are some hints that can help you to write a strong topic sentence.

Characteristics of a Topic Sentence

STEP 1. A TOPIC SENTENCE SHOULD SET THE STAGE FOR WHAT YOU PLAN TO SAY IN THE PARAGRAPH. In order to do this, a topic sentence makes a statement that will be explained or supported throughout the paragraph. Once the statement has been made, you can decide what ideas you need to support it. Look at the following paragraph.

> *Some bosses can be a pain in the neck!* Some don't keep their word. Others lie. Some are not concerned about their mistakes. They simply look for a scapegoat to take the blame. Others get upset if anyone else makes a decision or draws attention. Bosses sometimes make fun of their employees, even in front of others. A few are sure they know it all! The list of unpleasant and unfair types of bosses could go on and on.

MODEL
Setting the Stage

The topic sentence sets the stage for the paragraph about certain types of bosses. It states that some bosses can be a problem. Each additional sentence adds a claim to support the idea in the topic sentence.

STEP 2. YOU CAN USE THE TOPIC SENTENCE TO EXPRESS YOUR PURPOSE. Your purpose in writing may be to share an experience or knowledge, issue a warning, explore an idea, or change someone's thinking or behavior. In other situations, you may want to describe someone or something, compare and contrast two or more things, give reasons, or explain a cause-and-effect relationship. Sometimes you will state the purpose directly. Sometimes you will imply it. In the paragraph about bosses, the writer didn't say, "My purpose is to give examples of difficult bosses," but from the first sentence you can grasp the writer's purpose.

STEP 3. YOU CAN USE THE TOPIC SENTENCE TO REVEAL YOUR ATTITUDE TOWARD THE TOPIC. An attitude can be serious, cynical, humorous, bitter, or joyful. In the paragraph about bosses, the writer's attitude is clearly negative about certain types of bosses. The tone of the topic sentence sets the stage for the statements that follow.

The tone of the topic sentence sets the stage for the statements that follow.

In the following paragraph, notice how the topic sentence
- sets the stage for the rest of the paragraph
- expresses the writer's purpose
- reveals the writer's attitude

MODEL
Purpose and Attitude

You are cordially invited to enjoy the many benefits of a charge account at Sears, Roebuck and Co. Like thousands of our customers, you'll appreciate the convenience of shopping without carrying cash. You'll also be able to shop by mail or telephone. Merchandise that you really need can be purchased now, and you can arrange to pay later. Finally, you'll be delighted with the personal attention we give our charge account customers.

The topic sentence in this model tells you that you will read about the benefits of a Sears charge account (*setting the stage*). The topic sentence also expresses the writer's purpose (*to invite you to open an account*) and reveals the writer's attitude (*positive and friendly*).

Exercise C: Selecting the Correct Topic Sentence

Below you'll find a list of topic sentences all related in some way to learning to drive. Beside these are several paragraphs without topic sentences. Select the paragraph that would best fit each topic sentence and write its letter in the space provided. Hints are given to help you choose the topic sentence that expresses the main idea of the sentences that will follow it.

Topic Sentences

1. While learning to drive, wise people protect themselves from accidents in several ways.
   (*Hint:* The rest of the paragraph will probably tell you the different ways people protect themselves.)
   Paragraph letter _____

Paragraphs

A. A learner's permit may be obtained at a special office usually called "The Registry," officially known as the Registry of Motor Vehicles. In order to qualify for a learner's permit, you must present proof of your age and pass a written test that covers laws and regulations concerning driving in your state.

2. There are as many types of driving teachers as there are models of cars.

(*Hint:* The rest of the paragraph will probably give you different descriptions of driving teachers.)
Paragraph letter _____

3. The first step in getting a driver's license is usually getting a learner's permit.

(*Hint:* The rest of the paragraph will probably tell you how to get a learner's permit.)
Paragraph letter _____

4. There are certain topics you can be pretty sure will be covered on the written driving test.

(*Hint:* The paragraph will probably tell you the topics that are likely to be on the test.)
Paragraph letter _____

5. Everyone should have to take a driver education course before obtaining a driver's license.

(*Hint:* The paragraph should tell you the reasons why everyone should take a driver education course.)
Paragraph letter _____

B. The Cadillac variety of driving teacher teaches you to park in expensive lots. The Chevrolet variety has a "Buy American" bumper sticker. Mine was the big Buick type—he was tall and waved an unlit cigar around.

C. Although it is true that most people can learn to drive with the help of a friend or relative, there is more to operating a car than just staying on the right side of the road. I am willing to bet that more accidents are caused by people who have never taken driver's education than those who have. Every state should require driver's education.

D. A very important precaution is taking your first few lessons in a large, empty parking lot where there is nothing to hit! It's also a good idea not to do any driving at rush hour when you're starting out. Narrow downtown streets are also dangerous for new drivers and should be avoided.

E. You should be able to tell the meaning of warning signs from their shapes and colors. You will need to know what the laws are concerning drunk driving. You will probably be asked who has the right-of-way at different types of intersections.

ANSWERS ARE ON PAGE 34.

Writing a Topic Sentence

When writing your own topic sentences, keep these goals in mind:

STEP 1. STATE THE TOPIC CLEARLY. To do this effectively, you must decide two things. First, what is the topic you want to discuss? Second, what is it that you want to say about this topic? For example, suppose you decide that you want to write about the mayoral election in your city. This is not enough information to write a topic sentence. What do you want to say about the mayoral election? that it was a landslide? that you were displeased with the outcome? that it was an important event in your city? Once you have decided what you want to say about your topic, you can write your topic sentence. For example:

Step 1. What is the topic? *the mayoral election*
Step 2. What do I want to say about it? *that it was a landslide*
TOPIC SENTENCE: The mayoral election was an enormous landslide.

OR

Step 1. What is the topic? *the mayoral election*
Step 2. What do I want to say about it? *that I am unhappy with the outcome*
TOPIC SENTENCE: I am unhappy with the outcome of the mayoral election.

OR

Step 1. What is the topic? *the mayoral election*
Step 2. What do I want to say about it? *that it is an important event and that people should treat it that way*
TOPIC SENTENCE: The mayoral election is an important event and should be treated as such.

Notice that each writer decided that the topic was the election of a mayor. Then each writer decided what to say about this election. These two decisions are the first steps in writing a good topic sentence.

STEP 2. USE A COMPLETE SENTENCE. The topic sentence must express a complete thought. It is not merely a heading or title. It cannot, therefore, be an incomplete sentence such as "The importance of diet" or "How to balance your checkbook." To strengthen your writing of complete sentences, work on Sentence Highlight #1. The Sentence Highlights presented in this and the following chapters will review the basic sentence concepts and skills you need to be an effective writer.

SENTENCE HIGHLIGHT #1

In this Highlight, we will review what makes up a complete sentence. To be complete, a sentence must have all three of the following characteristics:

1. It must have a subject (the subject tells you whom or what the sentence is about).
2. It must have a predicate (the predicate must contain a verb and tell you something about the subject).
3. It must express a complete thought. (The words between the first capital letter and the end punctuation must give you some complete information.)

George Melican   got married.
subject   *predicate*
(Who?)   (What about him?)

The sentence above gives you some information you did not have before. You now know that George Melican got married.

Aerobic dancing   can be strenuous fun!
subject   *predicate*
(What?)   (What about it?)

The sentence above gives you some information about aerobic dancing. This is a complete sentence.

A group of words that does not have these three characteristics is not a sentence and is called a *fragment*. The group of words here is a fragment because it does not contain a predicate.

My son, the electrical engineer.
            subject   (What about the son?)

This group of words is not a sentence because it does not have a subject.

Went to court for a traffic violation.
predicate   (Who went to court?)

This group of words is not a sentence because it does not express a complete thought. You have no new information after reading the words.

Because my library books were overdue.

(What happened because the books were overdue? What about it? Were you fined? Did you hurry to the library?)

To make this group of words a sentence, add words to make a complete thought.

Because my library books were overdue, I hurried to return them.

Sentence Highlight Exercise 1

In the two paragraphs below, some of the sentences are complete and some are incomplete (fragments). In the spaces provided, write "sentence" if the group of words is a complete sentence or "fragment" if the group is an incomplete sentence. Each group of words is numbered in the paragraph.

REMEMBER: A complete sentence has a subject and a predicate, and it expresses a complete thought.

A. ¹Two day care centers are located nearby. ²One close to the factory on 25th St. where I work. ³It is expensive. ⁴The kids get to do lots of special activities. ⁵When I get promoted to supervisor. ⁶I will take my daughter Elena there. ⁷Now goes to a place where the kids are cooped up inside all day.

1. *Sentence*   5. _____

2. *fragment*   6. _____

3. _____   7. _____

4. _____

B. ¹You should tell the customer. ²How to put on the storm window. ³She should raise the inside window. ⁴Then she should push in the white plastic tabs. ⁵At the lower edge of the screen. ⁶Then she should push the screen up past its frame. ⁷Then the storm window in the slot where the screen was.

1. _____   5. _____

2. _____   6. _____

3. _____   7. _____

4. _____

ANSWERS AND EXPLANATIONS ARE ON PAGE 35.

Exercise D: Writing a Topic Sentence

Read each of the following paragraphs and write a good topic sentence for each one. To write the topic sentence, first ask yourself what the topic is and then what is being said about the topic. Use the hints in Sentence Highlight #1 to make sure you have a complete sentence.

1. Topic Sentence: _____

_____

_____

Right now the policy says that employees who don't use their sick days aren't able to use them as vacation days. As a result, some employees call in sick just to get a day off, making other workers resentful. It would certainly be fairer if people who haven't used their sick days were allowed to take a day or two off.

2. Topic Sentence: _____

_____

_____

Softball is played with a ball that is bigger and softer than a standard baseball. The bases are closer together, and the bats are a lighter weight. However, the rules are very much like those in baseball.

3. Topic Sentence: _____

_____

_____

It takes skill to fell the tree properly and time to cut it into stove-size lengths. Then, splitting the logs is quite a chore, especially if you aren't used to that kind of work. Finally, stacking it makes your body burn a lot of calories.

4. Topic Sentence: _____

_____

_____

Local businesses certainly have enough extra money to help us out. Since these businesses are part of our community, they should take some of the responsibility for fixing up public areas. With our organization and their funding, we could really make Stanley Park beautiful again!

5. Topic Sentence: _____

_____

_____

She is frequently late for work, and she doesn't seem to be interested in her job. Whenever she is given a new project to start, she grumbles and looks miserable. Maybe we should move Dorota into a position better suited to her interests.

POSSIBLE ANSWERS ARE ON PAGES 35 AND 36.

Exercise E: Writing More Topic Sentences

Imagine that you are in each situation given below and have been asked to write a paragraph for each purpose. Think about what your topic sentence would be by (1) deciding on your topic and (2) deciding what you want to say about that topic. Write these thoughts down. Then write your topic sentence on the lines provided. Remember, you are writing a complete sentence, not a title.

EXAMPLE: You are filling out an application for a job at the Post Office. One section asks you to write about your work experience. Your purpose is *to give work experience.*

Topic: *My work experience*

What I want to say about it: *I have learned a variety of skills.*

Topic Sentence: *Through my work experiences, I have learned a wide variety of social skills.*

1. The Internal Revenue Service sent you a letter saying you did not pay enough in taxes last year. You are sure you did. You decide to write back to the IRS. Your purpose is *to tell about your disagreement over taxes due.*

Topic: _____

What I want to say about it: _____

Topic Sentence: _____

_____

2. You are leaving your children with a new babysitter, and you want to leave a note telling her what to do in case of an emergency. Your purpose is *to tell the babysitter what to do if there is an emergency.*

Topic: _____

What I want to say about it: _____

Topic Sentence: _____

_____

3. The school you are applying to requires you to fill out an admissions application. Section II asks you what your career goals are. Your purpose is *to explain your career goals.*

   Topic: _____

   What I want to say about it: _____

   Topic Sentence: _____

   _____

4. Your employer asks you to get a medical checkup. You go to Dr. Smith for the first time. He asks you to write a brief medical history of yourself. Your purpose is *to give your personal medical history.*

   Topic: _____

   What I want to say about it: _____

   Topic Sentence: _____

   _____

5. After buying a can of ravioli and opening it, you found it to be spoiled. You decide to write to the manufacturer to report it. Your purpose is *to complain about a product.*

   Topic: _____

   What I want to say about it: _____

   Topic Sentence: _____

   _____

6. Your brother writes to you and asks for a loan. Your finances are low right now. You reply to him. Your purpose is *to refuse to loan money.*

   Topic: _____

   What I want to say about it: _____

   Topic Sentence: _____

   _____

7. A catalog mail-order company sent you the wrong color merchandise. You want to send it back with a letter explaining the problem. Your purpose is *to exchange merchandise.*

Topic: _____

What I want to say about it: _____

Topic Sentence: _____

_____

POSSIBLE ANSWERS ARE ON PAGES 36 AND 37.

Placement of Topic Sentence

Where in the paragraph should you place the topic sentence? It is possible to put the topic sentence anywhere in a paragraph. A skillful writer might put it at the end or even in the middle. A writer might even imply rather than state the main idea. But in general, and especially for the inexperienced writer, the most effective place to put the topic sentence is at the beginning of the paragraph. Placing it at the beginning helps both you and your reader. First, it forces you to pinpoint your main idea. Then, it helps you to keep the rest of your sentences on track. It also clearly tells your reader what to expect.

What Is the Relationship of the Topic Sentence to the Paragraph?

Paragraphs develop the idea presented in the topic sentence. In other words, the topic sentence gives a paragraph its focus. The topic sentence holds the details together in a way that lets us understand their importance and meaning.

Here is a paragraph without a topic sentence. It is confusing. The reader probably will not understand what it is about.

> There may be an underlying disease, such as high blood pressure. But in many cases there is no disease. Some people are affected following exercise, colds, or exposure to high altitude. The bleeding usually is more annoying than serious. Occasionally the bleeding is great, long lasting, and dangerous.

Now read the same paragraph with a topic sentence.

> *Nosebleeds may occur for no apparent reason or as a result of injury.* There may be an underlying disease, such as high blood pressure. But in many cases there is no disease. Some people are affected following exercise, colds, or exposure to high altitude. The bleeding usually is more annoying than serious. Occasionally the bleeding is great, long lasting, and dangerous.

The second paragraph is much easier to understand. We know for sure what the main idea is. Think of the whole paragraph as a table. The topic sentence is the tabletop, and the supporting sentences are the legs. Without the tabletop, you do not have a complete paragraph. With the tabletop in place, you can see what main idea the legs are supporting.

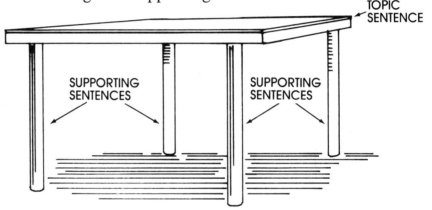

Of course, a topic sentence without any supporting sentences would also not be a paragraph, just as a tabletop with no legs to stand on would not be a real table.

The relationship of the topic sentence to the paragraph is, therefore, a two-way relationship. The topic sentence is an all-inclusive sentence. It is like an open umbrella. Under it come all the supporting sentences. Any idea that doesn't fit under that umbrella shouldn't be included. You may need a larger umbrella, one that will cover all the details.

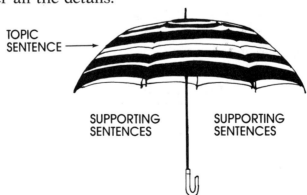

Your topic sentence should be the broadest, most general sentence in your paragraph. It sums up all the supporting sentences.

The paragraph below has a topic sentence that is not all-inclusive. Instead of helping the reader recognize the paragraph's main idea, it may be confusing.

> *Jean, you should come to live here because you would be such a great help to me.* You could help me with Tony before he goes to school in the mornings. You could stay with him when I have to work late. You and I would have time to spend together. Also, you would be able to get around more easily than from where you live now.

The topic sentence prepares us for a paragraph that develops the idea that Jean will be a great help. But the supporting sentences don't stick to that idea. Some have no relationship to helping at all. In this paragraph, the "umbrella" of the topic sentence does not cover all of the supporting ideas. The topic sentence is too narrow. The main idea that the supporting sentences <u>do</u> support is that there will be many advantages if Jean moves. A good topic sentence for this paragraph would be:

> *Jean, there would be many advantages for both of us if you moved in here.*

It is necessary to write a topic sentence that is broad enough to include all the details. But the topic sentence should also be narrow enough to define the boundaries of the paragraph. Look at the details in this paragraph and decide whether the topic sentence is as specific as it should be.

> *I would like to take classes at Clayton Community School because it is a good school.* The accounting department has an excellent reputation, and I plan to take all my courses in this department. Since my main areas of interest lie in this field, I feel that Clayton is the best choice for me. Having taken the beginning bookkeeping class and Accounting I and II, I feel I will be able to look for work in an accounting office.

The topic sentence of this paragraph states that the writer wants to take classes at Clayton because it is a good school. With this topic sentence, you might expect to find supporting sentences that give different examples of what is good about the school. Instead, you find three sentences that are all related to one aspect of the school—the accounting department. In this example, the writer made the topic sentence <u>too broad</u>. It should be rewritten to emphasize the accounting department of the school. For example:

> *I would like to take classes at Clayton Community School because of its excellent accounting department.*

This topic sentence defines the boundaries of the paragraph. It "sets the stage" for the supporting sentences that follow. This is a much better topic sentence than the broad sentence you saw in the first paragraph.

Exercise F: Broad vs. Narrow Topic Sentences

Each topic sentence in the paragraphs below is either too broad or too narrow. In other words, it does not define the supporting sentences that follow it. Read each paragraph and write "B" if the topic sentence is too broad or "N" if it is too narrow. Then rewrite the topic sentence so that it accurately defines what the paragraph is about.

1. *We have a lot of machines today.* When one of these machines breaks, we are often left groping for answers. How much will the repair cost? How long will it take? Can we be sure the job will be done correctly? Usually there are only two ways to solve the problem. We can either pay out lots of money to a repair shop or try to fix it ourselves.

   _____

   _____

2. *People use lists.* When you are trying to remember something, a list jogs the memory. Parties, grocery shopping trips, and odd jobs are often organized by lists. For some reason, lists enable people to keep schedules and get more done.

   _____

   _____

3. *Woodlake Homes offers many opportunities for the swinging single.* First of all, the three-bedroom ranch has plenty of space for a growing family. Second of all, nearby shopping malls and public transportation are great for retired people. Children will love our beautiful parks and playgrounds.

   _____

   _____

4. *It's time to make some changes.* A zesty taco plate for only $2.49 will spice up our lunch menu. A Greek salad will add a light touch to our dinner selections at only $3.75. And I'd like to see us add an exotic idea or two to our burger options—avocado on a California burger, for example.

_____

_____

5. *I hope you'll consider my son for the scholarship to Circle Center Academy because he is very bright.* He has made straight A's in school for the past two years. He is also a star on the soccer team. He can also sing beautifully and has been in our church choir for five years.

_____

_____

ANSWERS AND POSSIBLE TOPIC SENTENCES ARE ON PAGE 37.

Chapter Checklist

A good topic sentence
- ☐ expresses the main idea of the paragraph
- ☐ unifies the paragraph
- ☐ reveals your purpose and attitude
- ☐ is a complete sentence

ANSWERS

Exercise A

1. P   The first sentence of this paragraph introduces the idea that a baby undoes, or takes apart, things as soon as she can move around. The second two sentences describe ways she does this.

2. NP   You can tell this is not a paragraph because it doesn't have one topic. The writer talks about Doug catching big trout, people liking to eat fish, and Doug liking to fish. Although all relate to fish or fishing, there is no central or unifying idea.

3. P   The main idea in this paragraph, stated in the first sentence, is that people should be able to pay home heating bills in equal installments throughout the year. The rest of the sentences support the argument.

4. P   This paragraph presents an idea in the first sentence, that Ana Maria was frustrated and irritated by what Manolo did, and then supports this idea by describing the situation.

5. NP   These sentences are all related to gardening, but there is no one unifying idea to tie them together. You can't tell what point the writer might be trying to make.

6. NP   These three sentences all mention TV. However, there is no topic sentence, and you can't be sure what the writer really wants to say about TV, sports, or educational programs.

7. P   This paragraph has a unifying idea—that a car is a good friend only as long as it runs. The rest of the sentences are supporting sentences.

8. NP   This group of sentences can fool you. It starts out with a good topic sentence, and the second sentence supports the first sentence. However, the third sentence does not relate to the previous two, so you know right then it's not a paragraph.

Exercise B

1. a. C   b. S   c. S   d. T
2. a. T   b. S   c. S   d. C
3. a. T   b. S   c. C   d. S
4. a. S   b. S   c. C   d. S   e. T
5. a. S   b. T   c. S   d. S   e. C

Exercise C

1. D
2. B
3. A
4. E
5. C

Sentence Highlight Exercise 1

A.

1. *Sentence*   The subject is *two day care centers*. The predicate is *are located nearby*. The sentence expresses a complete thought.

2. *Fragment*   There is no verb in this sentence. You could correct it by writing "One *is* close to the factory on 25th St. where I work."

3. *Sentence*   The subject is *it*, and the predicate is *is expensive*.

4. *Sentence*   The subject is *the kids*, and the predicate is *get to do lots of special activities*. The sentence expresses a complete thought.

5. *Fragment*   There is a subject, *I*, and a predicate, *get promoted to supervisor*. However, there is no complete thought. When I get promoted to supervisor, *then what?*

6. *Sentence*   The subject is *I*, and the predicate is *will take my daughter Elena there*. A complete thought is expressed.

7. *Fragment*   There is no subject. You could correct it by saying "Now *she* goes to a place where the kids are cooped up inside all day."

B.

1. *Sentence*   The subject is *you*, and the predicate is *should tell the customer*. A complete thought is expressed.

2. *Fragment*   There is no complete thought. What about *how to put on the storm window?*

3. *Sentence*   The sentence has a subject, *she*, a predicate, *should raise the inside window*, and expresses a complete thought.

4. *Sentence*   The subject is *she* and the predicate is *should push in the white plastic tabs*. It expresses a complete thought.

5. *Fragment*   This one has neither a subject nor a verb. What is *at the lower edge of the screen?*

6. *Sentence*   The subject is *she*. The predicate is *should push the screen up past its frame*. There is a complete thought.

7. *Fragment*   This one has no verb. You could correct it by writing "Then the storm window *goes* in the slot where the screen was."

Exercise D

The answers given here are models that you can compare your answer to. Your topic sentence may look very different. Does your answer state both what the topic is and what you want to say about it? Is it a complete sentence?

1. The writer is presenting an argument about a company policy regarding sick days and making a suggestion that it should be changed. A good topic sentence might be:

    I don't think our company's policy on sick days is fair.

    OR

    Our company should change its policy on sick days.

2. The writer is describing the differences and similarities between baseball and softball. A good topic sentence would be:

    > Baseball and softball are similar but not exactly alike.

3. The writer is describing the skill and muscle it takes to turn a tree into firewood. A good topic sentence would be:

    > Preparing firewood is not easy.

4. The paragraph is about asking businesses to contribute to the fixing up of a public park. A good topic sentence would be:

    > Our park project needs a good source of money in the local business community.

    > OR

    > Businesses are our best prospect for finding money to fix up Stanley Park.

5. The writer is telling about a worker who does not seem to be satisfied with her job and is suggesting a solution. A good topic sentence would be:

    > Dorota doesn't seem to be happy working here, and I want to be sure we don't lose her.

Exercise E

The answers given here are models that you can compare your answer to. Be sure that your sentence states the topic clearly and lets the reader know what you're going to say about it. Also be sure that it's a complete sentence.

1. **topic:** disagreement over taxes due
    what I want to say about it: that I can prove that I paid enough taxes
    topic sentence: I have re-checked my financial records for the past year, and I can prove that I have paid the right amount of taxes.

2. **topic:** what to do in an emergency
    what I want to say about it: call the neighbor and ask for help
    topic sentence: In case there's any emergency, call Mr. Webster next door for help.

3. **topic:** my career goals
    what I want to say about it: that I want to own a dairy farm
    topic sentence: My career goal is to some day own my own dairy farm.

4. **topic:** my medical history
    what I want to say about it: our family history of heart disease, my current sinus condition, and my back problems are important
    topic sentence: The most important items in my medical history are my family history of heart disease, my sinus condition, and my persistent back pain.

5. **topic:** the ravioli I bought
   what I want to say about it: it was spoiled
   topic sentence: I was very angry when I opened a can of your brand of ravioli and found that it was spoiled.

6. **topic:** loaning money to my brother
   what I want to say about it: I can't afford to
   topic sentence: I'm sorry to tell you that I can't afford to loan you any money right now.

7. **topic:** the merchandise I ordered
   what I want to say about it: you sent the wrong color
   topic sentence: I would like to exchange this pair of pants since I ordered green but you sent red.

Exercise F

The sentences given here are examples of good topic sentences for the paragraphs. The topic sentences you wrote may be different. Look back at the Chapter Checklist and see if your topic sentences have these characteristics.

1. B   We depend a great deal on machines today.

2. B   Lists are very helpful in organizing your life.

3. N   Woodlake Homes has something for everyone.

4. B   Some jazzy additions to our menu will keep our customers interested.

5. N   I hope you'll consider my son for the scholarship to Circle Center Academy because he has so many talents.

3. Writing a Whole Paragraph

Unity and the Topic Sentence

In the last chapter, you learned that a paragraph is a series of sentences developing a single topic or idea. All of the sentences in the paragraph should work together to make the main idea clear.

Here is a series of sentences whose main idea is unclear.

> Plastic taped over the edges of windows can insulate against gusts of wind. You can cover your hot water heater with a quiltlike sleeve to keep warmth in. In addition, hardware stores carry different kinds of weatherstripping for doorjambs and floorboards, and an employee there can easily tell you how to use it.

Exactly how these sentences are related is unclear. What is missing? A topic sentence is needed to give them unity. Here are the same sentences with a topic sentence added.

MODEL
Unity

> *Winterizing your home to keep your utility bills down is easy and inexpensive.* Plastic taped over the edges of windows can insulate against gusts of wind. You can cover your hot water heater with a quiltlike sleeve to keep warmth in. In addition, hardware stores carry different kinds of weatherstripping for doorjambs and floorboards, and an employee there can easily tell you how to use it.

Adding a topic sentence clarifies the main idea of the sentences. With a good topic sentence to tie the ideas together, we now know that the paragraph is discussing easy ways to winterize your home.

Of course, the topic sentence is not the only element that gives unity to a paragraph. In this unit, you will see how to add supporting sentences that unite ideas in your paragraph. First, though, try unifying the ideas in the following exercise.

Exercise A: Writing a Topic Sentence

For each item below, read the ideas given. Then write a topic sentence that makes the main idea of the sentences clear.

1. _____

   You can trade in your old one in return for a lower price.
   There are also many makes, models, and colors to choose from.
   Payments can be spread out over four years, or the sticker
      price can be paid in one lump sum.
   In addition, you must decide how much you can afford to
      spend.

2. _____

   Marshall Lind felt like a drowned rat.
   Jets of water were squirting in every direction.
   The wrench had poked holes in the pipe in three places.
   Surely there were better ways to spend a Saturday.

3. _____

   She was never able to please her high school speech teacher.
   When she was asked to speak at a club meeting, she shook all
      over.
   She got off to a good start one time at a PTA meeting but
      began to stammer.
   Diane sometimes even felt sick to her stomach when she was
      asked her opinion.

4. _____

Lon has fond memories of all the trips they've been on
   together.
He washes, waxes, and polishes the van with great care.
He is sure other people become emotionally attached to their
   Volkswagens.
He often thinks of the times he used the van for work.

5. _____

For three years now, Marla had been careful to do the best
   work possible.
Marla Clark's boss told her she was going to be replaced.
Marla tried to think of even one thing she had done wrong.
The boss had acted strangely when he handed her the last
   paycheck.

6. _____

Ventura was sure the evidence proved that José Santiago was
   guilty.
He had gotten lots of mail from people who claimed José was
   innocent.
Judge Ventura went ahead and made the decision to proceed
   with José's trial.
For many months after the trial, he continued to get
   threatening phone calls.

7. _____

There are some citizens who favor allowing prayer in the public
   schools.
A great number of people feel the government should not
   legislate religion.
This issue of prayer in the public schools has driven a wedge
   between liberals and conservatives.
The issue even pits liberals against liberals and conservatives
   against conservatives.

POSSIBLE TOPIC SENTENCES ARE ON PAGE 65.

Unity and Supporting Sentences

As you just saw, the topic sentence has a lot to do with whether or not a paragraph has unity. But the topic sentence alone doesn't assure that a paragraph is unified. In addition, the supporting sentences in a paragraph must all be related to the topic sentence.

You already know the purpose of a topic sentence. The topic sentence makes the main idea clear to your readers. The purpose of the supporting sentences is to develop, explain, describe, or prove the topic sentence. The following steps will help you write clear supporting sentences.

STEP 1. BRAINSTORM FROM A TOPIC SENTENCE. You **brainstorm** to come up with the ideas that support your topic sentence. Once you have decided what you want to write about, you then have to communicate something about it to your readers. For example, if your topic is the many differences between living in a city and living in a suburb, you'll want to jot down the differences that come to mind. If your topic sentence says that the city should put up a new traffic light at your corner, you'll probably scribble down several reasons you think this should be done. Since it is a good idea to start with paragraphs that are about six sentences long, you should write down at least five ideas that support your topic sentence.

Start brainstorming by writing down your topic sentence at the top of a blank sheet of paper. List the main supporting points you can think of. Using simple words and phrases, jot down the ideas just as they come to mind. While brainstorming, don't worry about writing the supporting points as complete sentences. Write your ideas down in any form that comes naturally to you. Also, you may not be absolutely sure that an idea is related to your topic sentence. Write it down anyway. Don't worry about the order of your supporting ideas either. Later in this chapter, you will learn how to organize your ideas. You will also have a chance to eliminate ideas that don't belong in the paragraph.

Look on the following page at the sample topic sentence and list of possible brainstorm ideas.

TOPIC SENTENCE: An elderly person who lives alone can benefit from adopting a pet.

Pet gets new home
elderly person spends a lot of time at home
my widowed grandmother has 3 cats
elderly person feels needed, wanted,
*   and loved*
elderly person doesn't feel so alone
large numbers of unwanted pets
*   are put to sleep each year*

Even though your brainstorm list should be flexible, every point should relate to the topic. You will have a chance later to decide whether or not to use each point in your final paragraph. Don't worry about making those decisions now.

When you try to create your own brainstorm list, you should give yourself between five and ten minutes. At first, it may be difficult for you to come up with enough ideas by yourself. Brainstorming can also be done in a group or with a partner. Your partner or partners may suggest ideas that you never thought of. Or, something your partner says may influence you to suggest a new idea. In that way, you may work off one another. You may then be able to use those ideas in your paragraph.

Use one of the topics below to practice brainstorming with a partner or group. Working together, see how many different ideas you can come up with. Remember, use simple words and phrases.

Dreams　　Television Ads　　Music

Did your partner or partners come up with good ideas? How were you able to work off one another's suggestions? You can work off your own suggestions, too. Once you get an idea on paper, more ideas will naturally occur to you. The important first step is to simply write down <u>everything</u>.

STEP 2. BRAINSTORM FROM A TOPIC. Sometimes, even though you know your topic, you may be unsure exactly how you feel about it. For example, your topic may be *recycling at your school or office.* You may think that recycling is a good idea, but that it will be hard to get everyone to participate. What is your main idea? How do you really feel about recycling? In such cases, you will not have a topic sentence to brainstorm from, so you may need more time to think. Don't panic! With a little time, you will still write a well-unified paragraph.

This time, start by writing your topic at the top of a blank sheet of paper. Use the topic of recycling. Then, just as before, write down simple words and phrases that relate to your topic. Under *recycling,* you might write details like "don't throw away newspapers" and "everyone should try to do their part." Don't worry about trying to unify your ideas yet. Just write down everything you can think of that relates to your topic. This time, do not limit yourself to five points. You want more than five ideas, because later you will have to combine some of the ideas and eliminate others.

Now you are ready to create your own brainstorm list from a topic sentence. Use the following exercise to see how many good ideas you can come up with by yourself.

Exercise B: Brainstorming from a Topic Sentence

Read the topic sentences given below and choose <u>two</u> to brainstorm from. Write down the topic sentences you chose and list your brainstormed ideas below them.

1. I am writing to you, Congresswoman Evans, because I feel that you can help me with my problem.

2. Basketball is a popular, fast-paced sport.

3. The use of seat belts would reduce the number of auto-related deaths and accidents.

4. I believe we need a designated smoking area in this office.

5. The store was filled with anxious shoppers.

6. It is a son's or daughter's duty to care for an aging parent.

A POSSIBLE BRAINSTORM LIST IS ON PAGE 65.

Look at the topic and brainstormed ideas below. Notice that the topic is similar to the topic sentence on page 42, but it is much more general.

TOPIC: Adopting a Pet

go to local animal shelter
fill out form
saves animal from being put to sleep
having some living thing to come home to every night
good for children to learn responsibility for
   taking care of something
good for lonely people, or people who live alone
wish I could adopt a pet, but my building
   doesn't allow pets
not good for someone who travels a lot
can get expensive
I would get a puppy or kitten

Did you notice that it is not clear how all of the ideas are related to one another? However, they do all relate to the *topic* of adopting a pet. Later, you will learn how to decide which ideas you want to use in your final paragraph. But for now, use Exercise C to come up with ideas from *general topics*.

Exercise C: Brainstorming from a Topic

Read the suggested topics written below and choose <u>two</u> to brainstorm from. Write down the topics you chose and list your brainstormed ideas below them.

1. this newspaper
2. your favorite restaurant
3. a recurring nightmare
4. exercising
5. giving money to a homeless person
6. computers in education (or in the workplace)

A POSSIBLE BRAINSTORM LIST IS ON PAGE 65.

STEP 3. CLUSTER FROM A TOPIC SENTENCE. Making a *list* of brainstormed ideas is not the only way to come up with details that support your topic or topic sentence. Another method that you can try is called **clustering**. When you **cluster**, you actually make a **cluster map**. Start by placing your topic sentence in a circle in the center of a blank page. Then, as you think of details that support this topic sentence (just as you did in brainstorming), attach them to your center circle. This method may be easier for people who like to learn by using visual aides.

Look at the example below of a cluster map.

TOPIC SENTENCE: I'd rather live alone than with a roommate.

What similarities do you see between a cluster map and a brainstormed list? What are the differences?

Notice that in a cluster map, sometimes one detail seems to come naturally after another. The detail "other people won't touch my stuff" seemed to go with "more privacy," so it was attached to it rather than to the center circle. This will help you in the organizing process later. But first, try Exercises D and E. In Exercise D, you will complete a cluster map that has already been started for you. You will have the chance to create your own cluster map in Exercise E.

Exercise D: Finishing a Cluster Map

Below is a cluster map that has already been started. There is room left for you to finish it. Add all the details that come to mind just as you do when you brainstorm. Remember, some of your ideas may be connected to one another.

TOPIC SENTENCE:

nose is constantly running

When I have a cold or the flu, I feel miserable.

just want to stay in bed

USE THE MODEL OF A CLUSTER MAP ON PAGE 45.

Exercise E: Making a Cluster Map from a Topic Sentence

Read the topic sentences listed below and choose two to make cluster maps from. Write the topic sentences in the center of your page and write your ideas around them.

1. Fast-food restaurants are very popular in the U.S.
2. I'd rather buy an American-made automobile than a foreign-made one.
3. Parents should help their children with their homework.
4. I want to tell you about my ideas for the company party.
5. I'm writing to protest the proposed raise in bus fares.
6. Movies are better in the movie theater than on TV.

A POSSIBLE CLUSTER MAP IS ON PAGE 66.

STEP 4. CLUSTER FROM A TOPIC. You must remember that sometimes when you write, you may know your topic (it may be assigned to you), but you need to come up with your own topic sentence. Remember the topic of recycling on page 43. You may not have been sure exactly how you felt about it. Using a cluster map can help you to think of many ideas about your topic and to decide your opinion of it. Begin a cluster map by writing your topic in a circle in the center of a blank page. Then, add all the details that come to mind around the center circle.

Look at the example below of a topic and cluster map.

TOPIC: Living with a roommate versus living alone

less privacy with roommate

different sleep patterns

hard for both to be neat

living alone vs. living with a roommate

living alone can get lonely

nice to have someone to talk to

rather live with a relative than a friend

someone to share rent and bills

Exercise F: Making a Cluster Map from a Topic

Read the topics listed below and choose <u>two</u> to make cluster maps from. Write the topics in the center of your page and <u>write</u> your ideas around them.

1. the Olympics

2. watching baseball on TV versus being at a live game

3. keeping in touch with old friends

4. the high cost of education today

5. buying a stereo or VCR

6. smoking

A POSSIBLE CLUSTER MAP IS ON PAGE 66.

Organizing Your Ideas

You now know how to take a topic or topic sentence and come up with ideas that develop, explain, describe, or prove your topic. You also have learned two helpful prewriting methods, **brainstorming** and **clustering**. But where do you go from here? There is one more important step before you begin to write.

That step is to organize your ideas. Take a second look at your brainstorm lists and cluster maps. Then, follow these steps for completing the prewriting process: (1) eliminate any ideas that do not directly relate to your topic or topic sentence, (2) make sure all your sentences are complete, and (3) come up with your own topic sentence if you don't already have one.

STEP 1. GET RID OF IRRELEVANT IDEAS. Relevant details unify your paragraph. To be relevant, an idea must support the topic sentence. For example, in the brainstorm list on page 42 concerning an elderly person adopting a pet, what ideas are irrelevant? In other words, what ideas do not support or explain the idea that an elderly person who lives alone can benefit from adopting a pet? The fact that the writer's widowed grandmother has three cats does not relate to or support the topic sentence. Also, the point that large numbers of unwanted pets are put to sleep each year has nothing to do with the topic sentence. Although both of these points may be true, they are not relevant to the main idea expressed in the topic sentence.

Pet gets new home

elderly person spends a lot of time at home

~~my widowed grandmother has 3 cats~~

elderly person feels needed, wanted,
         and loved

elderly person doesn't feel so alone

~~large numbers of unwanted pets~~
         ~~are put to sleep each year~~

When you come across an irrelevant idea in your brainstorm list or cluster map, simply cross it out. It is not unusual to have several ideas on your list that you later decide not to use. Don't forget that when you brainstormed you wrote down what first came to mind. Now is the time to sort through all of these ideas and choose only those that suit your purpose.

Exercise G will allow you to practice spotting ideas that are not relevant to the topic sentence.

Exercise G: Finding Irrelevant Ideas

Read each topic sentence and brainstorm list below. Cross out the two ideas that do not support the topic sentence.

1. Above-ground swimming pools are more widely owned than in-ground pools for a number of reasons.

   relatively inexpensive

   pools are a plus in the summer   can be installed by a do-it-yourselfer

   can be taken down should the owner decide to move

   chlorine should be put in all pools

   maintenance easier

2. On the night the storm broke, Jan woke several times with her heart pounding in her throat.

   thought the roof was about to cave in
   building shuddered
   wind hammered against it
   beautiful weather in Atlanta   she'd always been afraid of storms
   Jan never went to sleep before 10:00

3. Moonlighting, or working a second job, can ruin a person's personal life.

   sleeping hours not regular
   meals get skipped   extra money sure can make things easier
   often makes one crabby with fellow workers
   night jobs are easier than day jobs
   family life suffers and often ends in divorce

4. Bill Kelly is as graceful as a five-legged elephant.

whenever he goes dancing, all the girls make themselves scarce

can't ride a bike

can't walk and talk at the same time

he does like to sleep a lot

once tripped over a chair on his way out of a room

likes to square dance

5. Being the child of divorced parents is not all bad.

two homes to go to instead of one

marriages seldom work out

parents don't fight anymore

brothers aren't happy about divorce

mother is a lot happier now

get to see each parent alone

6. I should quit this job.

low pay
no paid vacation

my father was a welder

no way to move up

boss too picky

hard to find another job

ANSWERS ARE ON PAGE 67.

STEP 2. DON'T BE FOOLED BY IDEAS THAT RELATE TO THE TOPIC BUT DO NOT SUPPORT THE TOPIC SENTENCE. For example, in the cluster map shown on page 45, the idea that the writer's brother has a good roommate may be true. This point does relate to the general topic of living with a roommate. But look again. Does this point support the topic sentence? Not really. The topic sentence is "I'd rather live alone than with a roommate." The writer's brother's roommate is not relevant.

When you are clustering or brainstorming and writing supporting sentences, it is important to keep in mind not only the topic, but also ***what you want to say about the topic.*** Remember that this was how you wrote your topic sentence as well. In the example above, the topic was living with a roommate. All of the ideas on the writer's cluster map were somehow related to this topic. But what is more important is ***what the writer said about this topic in the topic sentence.*** It is this statement that all the sentences on the brainstorm list should support.

In Exercise H you will have a chance to practice with ideas that relate to a general topic but do not support the topic sentence. This will help you eliminate irrelevant ideas from your paragraph.

When you are finished with Exercise H, go back to the cluster map on page 45. Cross out the ideas that are not relevant to the topic sentence.

Exercise H: Supporting the Topic Sentence

On the next page you will find a series of topics, topic sentences, and brainstorm ideas beside them. In each case, all of the brainstorm ideas relate to the general topic but not all of them support the topic sentence. Cross out those ideas that relate to the general topic, but do not support the topic sentence.

1. Topic: THE SOCIAL SECURITY SYSTEM

   Topic Sentence: Fifteen to twenty years from now there won't be any money left for Social Security funds.

   a. The elderly people of our country will be especially hard hit by the lack of funds.
   b. Almost everyone who has a job pays into the system through payroll deductions.
   c. The current administration is not taking action to preserve the Social Security system.
   d. Currently, more money is being paid out in benefits than is being taken in.
   e. Employees of certain types of institutions do not pay Social Security taxes.

2. Topic: PHYSICAL FITNESS

   Topic Sentence: Celebrity exercise videos, seen on millions of American TVs, have greatly contributed to making physical fitness fun rather than drudgery.

   a. Music and dancing have become standard in exercise classes.
   b. People can exercise along with the program right in their living rooms.
   c. Exercise clothing is one of the hottest fashion ideas these days.
   d. Each celebrity uses his or her personality, humor, and lots of encouragement to make the tapes fun.
   e. Everyone from ten-year-old children to adults in their sixties can do the exercises shown on the videos.

3. Topic: PARENTING

   Topic Sentence: The rewards of being a parent are greater than the disadvantages.

   a. Your children will teach you a lot about people.
   b. The schools in this neighborhood are pretty good.
   c. My mother says I was a happy baby.
   d. Watching an infant take a first step is an unforgettable experience.
   e. Playing with children gives you a chance to be creative.

4. Topic: GARBAGE DISPOSAL

Topic Sentence: I am writing to let you know how dissatisfied I am with the garbage disposal system in our neighborhood.

a. We have a pickup only once a week.

b. The drivers arrive at 5:30 A.M., before any of us have time to get our barrels out to the street.

c. Our building is on its last legs anyway.

d. I can't carry the garbage outside by myself.

e. The streets are covered with trash that spilled from the truck.

f. Our taxes should pay for better service than this.

5. Topic: LAW ENFORCEMENT

Topic Sentence: The Crime Stoppers program has served as an aid to state law enforcement officers.

a. Crime statistics have dropped in the counties where the program is being tried.

b. Crime is a growing problem in large cities.

c. In the program, volunteers serve as night patrollers in their cars.

d. Some young people now want to become police officers.

e. Volunteer counselors work with crime victims to encourage them to cooperate with police and press charges.

6. Topic: TELEPHONE BILLS

Topic Sentence: The telephone bill I received for the month of May was $2.97 more than I actually owe, and I would like credit.

a. I was charged $1.97 for a call to Detroit that I never made.

b. My monthly service fee should be $12.50, not $13.50.

c. Daytime calls are outrageously expensive.

d. Your repair service is slow and unreliable.

e. Please make the correction and credit me on my next bill.

ANSWERS ARE ON PAGE 67.

STEP 3. MAKE COMPLETE SENTENCES FROM YOUR IDEAS. Now that we have gone over the brainstorm list (page 42) and cluster map (page 45) to eliminate those ideas that didn't support the topic sentence, the ideas that remain will become the supporting sentences of the paragraphs.

Look at the paragraphs below, which were written from the brainstorm list and cluster map you saw on pages 42 and 45. Notice that the irrelevant ideas have been left out and that all sentences are complete.

> *An elderly person who lives alone can benefit from adopting a pet.* Many elderly people spend a great deal of time at home. They can use that time to take care of a pet. With a pet to love and care for, the elderly person is sure to feel needed and wanted. Because there is an active, living thing in the home, the elderly person won't feel so alone between visits from friends and family.

> *I'd rather live alone than with a roommate.* I like my privacy, so I don't like it when other people touch my stuff. I alone control the noise level in the apartment. It's quiet when I want to study, and I don't have to worry about making too much noise early in the morning or late at night. Also, I don't have to share anything with anyone. I have my own bathroom and my own telephone.

MODELS
Brainstorm or Cluster to Paragraph

SENTENCE HIGHLIGHT #2

The purpose of this Highlight is to review two sentence patterns that are built from simple sentences. Using these patterns can improve the effectiveness of your writing in two ways: (1) they can help express your ideas more precisely; and (2) they can make your writing style smoother.

1. The first pattern connects two simple sentences (coordination). You will use a comma and a logical coordinating word to connect the sentences.

COORDINATING WORDS: *and, but, for, or, nor, so, yet*

Notice how using these words makes your writing less choppy. It also helps make the relationship between ideas clear.

We tested the computer's printer.

That still didn't locate the problem.

We tested the computer's printer, **but** that still didn't locate the problem.

I couldn't afford night school tuition.

I asked for a small raise.

I couldn't afford night school tuition, **so** I asked for a small raise.

Ted Kessel leased a new apartment.

He got permission to repaint the living room and kitchen.

Ted Kessel leased a new apartment, **and** he got permission to repaint the living room and kitchen.

I will finish the shoe inventory.

I will put up the new window display.

I will finish the shoe display, **or** I will put up the new window display.

2. The second pattern also connects two simple sentences. In the process, however, this pattern changes one sentence. It makes one sentence less important (dependent) by giving it less emphasis. You will use a subordinating word to start the less emphasized part of the sentence.

SUBORDINATING WORDS:	USE:
because since so that in order to	to show the reason for something
whereas although though as though as if in spite of the fact that despite the fact that	to show contrast
before after while when as soon as as long as until	to express a time relationship
if unless	to express the conditions under which something may happen

Place a comma after a dependent clause when it starts the sentence.

I joined a record club.

I began ordering records like mad.

When I joined a record club, I began ordering records like mad.

He could attend his sister's wedding.

I traded work shifts with John.

So that he could attend his sister's wedding, I traded work shifts with John.

When the dependent clause comes after the main statement, do not place a comma between the two parts of the sentence.

Sharon is never on time to exercise class.

She usually overbooks herself.

Sharon is never on time to exercise class **because** she usually overbooks herself.

I tabulated the results of the survey.

I wrote the sales proposal.

I tabulated the results of the survey **before** I wrote the sales proposal.

Subordinating the idea of one sentence and connecting it to another is an especially effective way to make idea relationships clear to your reader. At the same time, occasional subordination gives your paragraph variety and a smoother style.

Sentence Highlight Exercise 2

On the first pair of lines, combine the short, choppy sentences using a logical coordinating word. Be sure to use a comma before the coordinating word. On the second set of lines, use a subordinating word to join the two sentences. Remember to use a comma when the dependent clause is first.

1. Meryl spent the afternoon looking for a new job.
   She could not find anything.

   Hint: *but*

   a. _____

   _____

   Hint: *Although*

   b. _____

   _____

2. My husband finally found a baby-sitter.
   We can come to your party after all.

   a. _____

   _____

   b. _____

   _____

3. The lawyers can come up with a better case.
   The defendant will go free.

   a. _____

   _____

   b. _____

   _____

4. Be sure to take those muffins out of the oven.
   They will burn.

   a. _____

   _____

   b. _____

   _____

5. Politicians will keep on abusing the public trust.
   We let it happen.

   a. _____

   _____

   b. _____

   _____

6. There is a shortage at the warehouse.
   You must contact the production manager immediately.

   a. _____

   _____

   b. _____

   _____

7. She had four cups of coffee.
   She finally went to work.

   a. _____

   _____

   b. _____

   _____

8. People are eating less meat than they used to.
Most restaurants offer some meatless alternatives.

a. _____

_____

b. _____

_____

9. Single-parent families are very common.
Day care facilities can't meet the demand in many cities.

a. _____

_____

b. _____

_____

ANSWERS ARE ON PAGE 67.

STEP 3. COME UP WITH YOUR OWN TOPIC SENTENCE. Remember that you still have some brainstorm lists and cluster maps that do not have topic sentences. You must take your ideas and come up with your own topic sentence.

For example, look again at the brainstorm list on page 44. The topic is adopting a pet. Do you see any ideas that are related and could be grouped together? Circle the ideas you think you could use in one paragraph. Or, draw arrows between related ideas. Use any method that makes the most sense to you. Then, look below at the copy of the brainstormed list from page 44. The writer circled the ideas he or she wanted to include in the paragraph.

go to a local animal shelter   can get expensive
fill out form
                                      I would get a puppy
save animals from being put to sleep   or a kitten

having some living thing to come home to every night

good for children to learn responsibility for taking
care of something

good for elderly people, or people who live alone
wish I could adopt a pet, but my building doesn't allow pets
not good for someone who travels a lot

Looking through the list, the writer found some good things that come from adopting a pet. The writer circled the details he or she wanted to include. The writer came up with this topic sentence and paragraph.

Adopting a pet can be very rewarding. When you adopt a pet from an animal shelter, you are saving that animal from being put to sleep. After you bring your new pet home, you have a living thing to come home to every night and meet you at the door. This is especially nice for someone who lives alone. Learning to take care of your new pet teaches both children and adults how to be responsible.

Now look at the cluster map on page 47. What ideas would you group together? What details would you eliminate? The writer decided there were more positive ideas about living with a roommate than about living alone. Look below at how the writer grouped together some ideas from the cluster map.

less privacy with roommate

living alone can get lonely

different sleep patterns

nice to have someone to talk to

living alone vs. living with a roommate

hard for both to be neat

someone to share rent and bills

rather live with a relative than a friend

someone to fix things

and help with chores

The writer grouped together the positive ideas and came up with this paragraph. Notice that a new idea was added even after the writer was through clustering.

There are many advantages to living with a roommate. Because you have a roommate, you won't get lonely. You'll always have someone to talk to. Your cost of living won't be too high because you can share the expenses, such as rent and utility bills. Your roommate can also help out by fixing things you cannot fix or doing a chore you dislike. Probably the best reason to live with a roommate, however, is that it teaches you how to live with other people just as you do when you get married and raise a family.

Chapter Checklist

A topic sentence	**Supporting sentences**
☐ Focuses topic	☐ Develop, explain, describe, or prove topic sentence
☐ Expresses main idea	☐ Are relevant to topic sentence
☐ Gives paragraph unity	☐ Are complete sentences
☐ Is a complete sentence	

Exercise I: Writing a Paragraph from a Topic Sentence

Choose two of the topic sentences below. First, make a brainstormed list or cluster map of ideas for each. Then select the points that support the topic sentence and cross out the others. Finally, complete the paragraph using the topic sentence and your ideas. Use the Chapter Checklist to make certain that each paragraph is complete. Write on every other line of your paper. This will help you in the editing phase later.

1. Many parents like "Sesame Street" because it offers joyful learning experiences for their children.

2. Please let me tell you the reasons I am qualified for this position.

3. Women are making quite an impact on the construction scene today.

4. I strongly recommend this book I have just finished, and here is why.

5. Changing a flat tire in the pouring rain is a real bummer.

6. Endless questions suddenly arise when two independent people decide to get married.

A MODEL PARAGRAPH IS ON PAGE 68.

Exercise J: Writing a Paragraph from a Topic

Select one topic from the list below. If you can, begin by writing a topic sentence. Next, write down a brainstorm list or cluster map and cross out irrelevant ideas. Finally, write a complete paragraph. Be sure to use the Chapter Checklists to make sure you have a well-organized paragraph.

1. teaching someone to drive

2. deciding to go back to school

3. drinking and driving

4. getting along with the boss

5. a popular TV program

6. people who pry into your personal life

A MODEL PARAGRAPH IS ON PAGE 68.

Portfolio Activity #1

This is the first of five portfolio activities. To help organize the activities, be sure to keep them all in a special folder called a **portfolio**. You and your instructor will pass this portfolio back and forth. Keeping your portfolio assignments together like this will help you and your instructor keep track of your progress.

You will be in charge of your own portfolio! The purpose of the portfolio is to give you a more active role in the evaluation and grading of your work. You will not only be the *writer*, but you will also be the *audience*, *editor*, and *grader*. By playing all these roles, you will learn how to judge the quality of your own writing. As you discover your strengths, weaknesses, and goals, you'll be able to improve your writing.

1. The most important part of a portfolio is that *you* choose the pieces you want to go in it. *You* decide what your best work is. Start now, by looking at your responses to Exercises I and J from Chapter 3. **Select the paragraph that interests you the most or that you are most proud of.**

   If you prefer, you may wish to write a completely new paragraph on something that interests you more. Try writing your new paragraph about an invention of the twentieth century that has made your life easier. Remember to start with a brainstorm list or cluster map. Also, be sure to write on every other line.

2. Next, remember to **save and include any prewriting materials** (brainstorm lists or cluster maps) **you create**. That way, both you and your teacher can see how you are coming up with your ideas.

3. Now, on top of your paragraph and prewriting materials, you will **attach one more page**. This will be the **cover page**. On your cover page, you will answer some questions in order to evaluate your writing.

   You may set up your cover page in a question-and-answer format, similar to the model on page 64. This model contains some questions that you should include as well as sample student answers. On your own cover page, try to answer the questions in complete sentences.

1. Briefly explain what the paragraph is about and what assignment you were responding to.

   My paragraph is about people who pry into my personal life. I chose topic #6 in Exercise J on page 62.

2. What was your purpose for writing this paragraph?

   My purpose was to explain why I don't like people who pry into my personal life.

3. Who is your intended audience?

   My intended audience is my teacher.

4. Where did you get your ideas from?

   I got my idea from my own personal experience in dealing with people.

5. What do you think is best about this paragraph? Why?

   I think the concluding statement is best because it sums everything up.

6. If you had more time, what would you work on?

   I would try to add a few specific examples.

7. When writing this paragraph, did you do anything different from what you have done to write a paragraph in the past?

   I spent ten minutes on a brainstorm list.

8. What kind of feedback do you want?

   I want to know if my paragraph seems complete or if something seems missing.

When you have gathered together your paragraph, your prewriting materials, and your completed cover page, you have finished this portfolio activity! Put all these materials into your portfolio, and turn it in to your instructor.

ANSWERS

Exercise A

Here are possible topic sentences for Exercise A. Yours will probably be a little different. Does your topic sentence unify all the ideas?

1. There are a lot of choices to make when you buy a new car.
2. The plumbing job was a disaster.
3. Diane was very afraid to speak in public.
4. Lon loves his Volkswagen van.
5. Marla Clark couldn't understand why she was fired from her job.
6. Judge Ventura made a very unpopular ruling on the Santiago case.
7. U.S. citizens continue to disagree on the issue of allowing prayer in the public schools.

Exercise B

There are no wrong answers in brainstorming. Did you write down everything you could think of that supported the topic sentence? Here is a sample brainstorm list for #4:

I believe we need a designated smoking area in this office.

some workers smoke, others don't
no one wants to give in totally to the others' demand
easy to separate smokers   my father died of
from non-smokers   cancer last year
clothes stink
health problems create productivity troubles
could use the back office as smoking area

Exercise C

Here is a sample brainstorm list for #2.

Topic: My Favorite Restaurant
Brainstorm List:

Angelina's Pizza   I love italian food
Pepperoni pizza and delicious minestrone soup
their pasta is not very good
not too expensive   nice waiters and
casual atmosphere   waitresses
my boyfriend used to work there
lots of locations throughout the city

Exercise E

Here is a sample cluster map for #6.

Topic Sentence: Movies are better in the theater than on TV.

TV movies are free

no commercials

movies are better in the movie theater than on TV

more exciting

big screen

Dolby stereo

movies are expensive

not edited

sex, violence swear words left in

may not be suitable for everyone

Exercise F

Here is a sample cluster map for #4.

Topic: The high cost of education today

textbooks are expensive

are teachers being paid too much or too little?

the high cost of education today

private school costs more

private colleges more expensive than state colleges

not all schools can afford computers

but students can get loans

Exercise G

You should have crossed out:

1. chlorine should be put in all pools
   pools are a plus in the summer

2. beautiful weather in Atlanta
   Jan never went to sleep before 10:00

3. extra money sure can make things easier
   night jobs are easier than day jobs

4. he does like to sleep a lot
   likes to square dance

5. brothers aren't happy about divorce
   marriages seldom work out

6. hard to find another job
   my father was a welder

Exercise H

You should have crossed out:

1. b, e
2. a, c
3. b, c
4. c, d
5. b, d
6. c, d

Sentence Highlight Exercise 2

Your answers will probably vary from these in some cases. Check to be sure that your answer makes sense and that you used a comma when one was needed.

1. a. Meryl spent the afternoon looking for a new job, but she could not find anything.
   b. Although Meryl spent the afternoon looking for a new job, she could not find anything.

2. a. My husband finally found a babysitter, so we can come to your party after all.
   b. Because my husband finally found a babysitter, we can come to your party after all.

3. a. The lawyers can come up with a better case, so the defendant will go free.
   b. Unless the lawyers can come up with a better case, the defendant will go free.

4. a. Be sure to take those muffins out of the oven, or they will burn.
   b. Be sure to take those muffins out of the oven because they will burn.

5. a. Politicians will keep on abusing the public trust, and we let it happen.
   b. Politicians will keep on abusing the public trust as long as we let it happen.

6. a. There is a shortage at the warehouse, so you must contact the production manager immediately.
   b. You must contact the production manager immediately because there is a shortage at the warehouse.

7. a. She had four cups of coffee, and she finally went to work.
   b. After she had four cups of coffee, she finally went to work.

8. a. People are eating less meat than they used to, so most restaurants now offer some meatless alternatives.
   b. Because people are eating less meat than they used to, most restaurants now offer some meatless alternatives.

9. a. Single-parent families are very common, and day care facilities can't meet the demand in many cities.
   b. Since single-parent families are very common, day care facilities can't meet the demand in many cities.

Exercise I

Here is a model that you can check your work against. Also be sure to use the Chapter Checklist to check your paragraph.

Topic Sentence: Endless questions suddenly arise when two independent people decide to get married.

Details: separate vs. joint checking accounts, whose apartment to live in or where to move to, what church (if any) to get married in . . .

Endless questions suddenly arise when two independent people decide to get married. For instance, they might be married in a church. Then they have to decide which church. They could combine their money in a joint account, or they could keep separate checking accounts. In addition, they could live in his apartment, or they could live in her apartment, or they could both move.

Exercise J

Here is a model paragraph that you can use to compare with your paragraph. Remember, regardless of which topic you write on, you should always have a strong topic sentence that states your purpose and five or so sentences that support your topic sentence. Use your Chapter Checklist to make sure your paragraph is a good one.

Topic: people who pry into your personal life

Topic Sentence: My least favorite kind of person is one who pries into my personal life.

Brainstorm List: my life is none of their business
when I need advice, I will ask for it
nosy people are seldom caring or thoughtful
Ted Ulmann is like that
like to keep work and family life separate
I am a pretty happy person

Paragraph: My least favorite kind of person is one who pries into my personal life. I just don't appreciate someone always asking a lot of questions. When I want advice or help, I will always ask for it. For the most part, I like to keep family and work life separate.

4. Paragraphs: Telling and Describing

The Purposes of Paragraphs

You can write different types of paragraphs, depending on what your purpose is. The paragraph you write can tell a story, describe, inform, or persuade. In this chapter we will first talk about the four different paragraph types and how each can be written most effectively. Then we will discuss telling a story and describing in particular. In Chapter 5, you will learn more about the other two types of paragraphs.

Paragraphs that tell a story are called **narrative** paragraphs. When telling the story, you may use some description or some explanation. The main purpose, though, is to ***tell what happened***.

Paragraphs that describe something are called **descriptive** paragraphs. In this type of paragraph, the writer describes a person, place, object, or event. The writer uses details that help the reader see, hear, touch, smell, and taste what is described. The main purpose of this paragraph is to ***help the reader get a picture of something***.

Paragraphs that inform or explain are called **informative** paragraphs. Informative paragraphs often include factual and descriptive details. The purpose of this type of paragraph is to ***explain something to the reader***. You will learn more about this type of paragraph in Chapter 5.

Paragraphs that try to persuade others to believe or behave in a certain way are called **persuasive** paragraphs. The writer states an opinion and then gives reasons to support it. The purpose of this type of paragraph is to ***give a point of view and support it***. You will learn more about persuasive writing in the next chapter.

Knowing your purpose for writing will help you to decide which of the four paragraph types you should use. For example, given a topic such as "choosing a family doctor," you must first decide on your purpose. Do you want to explain the process of choosing a family doctor (informative)? Do you want to tell a story about the time you chose your doctor (narrative)? Or do you want to persuade someone that one method of choosing is better than another (persuasive)?

The models below show how paragraphs on the same general subject can differ when written for different purposes. The topic is "discrimination on the job." A writer may want to tell what happened when she was due for a promotion and did not get it.

MODEL
Narrative

> *I once was a salesperson for a plumbing products company.* When the job of sales manager came open, I was clearly in line for the promotion. The vice president of our division even asked me to apply! Then, it was announced that a new man was being hired from outside the company for the job. I suddenly realized that they had intended to hire a man all along. They only pretended to consider me so it would look fair.

With the same general topic, another writer may have a completely different reason for writing. He may want to describe his feelings about being discriminated against.

MODEL
Descriptive

> *At my company, white guys who don't know what they're doing always get promoted into the skilled maintenance jobs.* It makes me really mad. I could do their jobs a lot better than they do. I have a good laugh when the residents ask for me, the janitor, when they need something fixed. But on payday, there's nothing to laugh about. I get tears in my eyes thinking about what I could give my family if I had the paycheck of a senior maintenance worker.

Another writer may, instead, want to inform the reader about a new antidiscrimination program in her company.

MODEL
Informative

> *Bethel Printing's new affirmative action program has three main points.* First, we will make sure that men and women who are doing the same jobs receive equal pay. Second, we will make sure that at least half of the people in our management training program are women. Third, when we are making hiring and promotion decisions, we will make every effort to move minorities and women into positions of responsibility.

In another situation, a writer may want to persuade someone that job discrimination is unfair.

> *It is unfair for employers to make any personnel decisions because of prejudice.* Think of the experienced female secretary who applies for the job of office manager. The company hires a man, denying her both an increase in salary and a career move. A competent, black store cashier applies for an entry-level position in management and is passed over. That cashier remains stuck in a low-paying job. It is true that prejudiced decisions like these hurt both the individual and the company.

MODEL
Persuasive

As you can see, it is possible to develop the same topic differently to suit different purposes. The topic sentence should be written after you have decided on your purpose and which of these four paragraph types you want to use. The topic sentence should indicate whether you intend to persuade, inform, describe, or tell a story. For example, the same topic of "my new apartment" can result in four very different topic sentences.

Descriptive:

My new apartment is larger and more modern than my last one.

Informative:

The lease for my new apartment states some upsetting renter's guidelines.

Narrative:

Let me tell you how I found my new apartment.

Persuasive:

You should forget living in the suburbs and rent a city apartment like mine.

Use the following exercise to practice recognizing the four different kinds of paragraph writing. Look at the topic sentence and the supporting sentences and see if you can figure out the writer's main purpose in writing the piece. As you do the exercise, you may refer to the list of paragraph types above.

Exercise A: Identify the Paragraph Type

Identify the paragraph type of each of the short paragraphs below. Does the paragraph inform, describe, persuade, or tell a story? Write the type of paragraph in the space given.

1. My daughter actually doesn't look much like me. She has lighter hair and darker eyes. Her skin tone is paler than mine, and her features are much sharper. People say that we have the same smile, but I think hers is prettier. Our builds are completely different, too. While I am close to six feet tall, she is barely over five.

   _____

2. Yesterday I went to the dentist to have a filling replaced. After the terrible drilling was done, Dr. Dickson pressed and tapped the filling into place, and off I headed for home. While on the way home, I unthinkingly popped a sticky gumdrop into my mouth and began chewing. Today I have another appointment with Dr. Dickson!

   _____

3. Of the one million girls between the ages of fifteen and nineteen who became pregnant last year, about one-third actually gave birth. Many of those girls who gave birth did so with the idea that the baby would somehow make them feel happier or help them get out of poverty. However, while having a child may be a joyful experience, it is rarely the answer to one's own personal problems.

   _____

4. Every taxpayer in the United States should take the time to find out where tax money is being spent. This should be a duty of every responsible citizen. Anyone who values the economy of a democracy must help to keep it running well. Monitoring the use of tax money is one way for citizens to take part in the government's economic good health.

   _____

5. The depressing sight of the burned-out apartment was enough to make Leroy sick to his stomach. The smoldering remains of his first real home stood out as a dreary scene against the cloudless blue sky. The bitter smell in the air burned his nostrils as he tried to make his way through the filthy heap. Leroy's pain soon turned to rising anger as he thought about who had done this.

   _____

6. When I finally got up the nerve to ask Loretta out, things actually went more smoothly than I had expected. I was able to get the right words out without looking too foolish, and my face didn't turn quite as red as it usually does. Before I was even able to finish saying what I wanted, Loretta nodded eagerly. Then she even suggested a place to go! As we walked toward the bus, we made plans to meet up, and before I knew it I had a date with the most terrific girl on Worthing Street!

7. Representative Solovay, please help me with a personal problem. I have been receiving public aid since June, when I was let go from my job at the supermarket. Because of my unemployment, my address has changed twice. Unfortunately, I have not received a check for December or January. I have repeatedly called the Department of Public Assistance but have gotten no answers about where my checks might be. Perhaps you will be able to help in this matter.

ANSWERS AND EXPLANATIONS ARE ON PAGE 92.

Exercise B: Writing Topic Sentences for the Four Types of Paragraphs

Seven topics are listed below. Choose any three topics and write a topic sentence for each type of paragraph listed. You will write nine topic sentences in all. Remember, to write a good topic sentence, first decide *what you want to say about the topic*. The topic sentence should reflect your purpose. If you are having trouble coming up with your purpose, make a brainstorm list or cluster map of ideas on a separate sheet of paper.

1. Topic: opening a savings account

   Persuasive topic sentence: _____

   _____

   Narrative topic sentence: _____

   _____

   Informative topic sentence: _____

   _____

2. Topic: playing the lottery

Narrative topic sentence: _____

_____

Descriptive topic sentence: _____

_____

Persuasive topic sentence: _____

_____

3. Topic: financing a child's education

Informative topic sentence: _____

_____

Descriptive topic sentence: _____

_____

Narrative topic sentence: _____

_____

4. Topic: filling out income tax forms

Descriptive topic sentence: _____

_____

Narrative topic sentence: _____

_____

Informative topic sentence: _____

_____

5. Topic: civil rights in your community

Informative topic sentence: _____

_____

Narrative topic sentence: _____

_____

Persuasive topic sentence: _____

_____

6. Topic: problem with locks on your apartment building or house

   Narrative topic sentence: _____

   _____

   Descriptive topic sentence: _____

   _____

   Persuasive topic sentence: _____

   _____

7. Topic: quitting school before graduation

   Narrative topic sentence: _____

   _____

   Informative topic sentence: _____

   _____

   Persuasive topic sentence: _____

   _____

POSSIBLE TOPIC SENTENCES ARE ON PAGES 92 AND 93.

Writing a Narrative Paragraph

As you saw above, paragraphs that tell what happens or tell a story are called **narrative paragraphs**. They relate a sequence of events, give the history of something, or tell about a single incident. The topic sentence of a narrative paragraph should reflect your purpose. In other words, when your reader reads your topic sentence, he or she should know that you plan *to tell what happened.*

Once you have your topic sentence, the next step is to brainstorm, just as you did in the previous chapter. Your brainstorm list for a narrative paragraph will probably be just a list of events that took place. Write down these events as they come to mind. Once you have completed your list, decide whether there are any ideas on it that are not important to your main point. If there are, cross them out as you did with irrelevant details in Chapter 3.

For example, look at the brainstorm list below and cross out those ideas that do not seem important enough to include in the paragraph.

Topic sentence: Rhonda's actions the two weeks before she was fired had the whole plant in an uproar.

late for work 6 days in a row

punched a co-worker   went to Bill's Pub after work

Thursday stole co-workers purse

next day she came in drunk

ruined bolts of cloth   cashed her last paycheck on lunch hour

You should have crossed out "went to Bill's Pub after work" and "cashed her last paycheck at lunch hour." Although both of these were events that took place, they are not important and do not support the topic sentence. They are not events that led to Rhonda's firing.

Sequence of Events

When you tell someone a story, you most likely start with what happened first, then second, etc. Your story is more easily understood that way. Similarly, events in a narrative paragraph are best developed in the same time order. This order is often called **sequence of events**. If you don't put the events in this order, your reader could become frustrated or completely confused. Imagine trying to understand the paragraph below if the sequence were scrambled instead of being put in order as the events happened.

> *I almost had an accident on my way home from work today!* It all happened so fast. **First**, as I approached an intersection, I pulled to a stop. **Then**, I glanced in my mirror and saw a huge red fire truck barreling down on me. The light was **still** red, and cross traffic was thick. What could I do? **When** I **next** looked in my rearview mirror, I saw the fire truck almost on me, siren **still** blaring, not slowing down. I cranked the wheel hard right and **finally** was able to move out in front of the cars to my right **just as** the fire truck went through.

MODEL
Narrative Paragraph

Words that connect the ideas in sentences are called **transition words**. Transition words, in dark type in the paragraph above, help the reader move smoothly from one idea to the next. These words are particularly important in paragraphs using time order, or sequence of events. They help the reader recognize and understand the story by adding signals to tell the order of things. In Sentence Highlight #3, you will see how this kind of transition word can be used in sentences to improve your paragraphs.

A good narrative paragraph
- has a topic sentence that reflects the purpose
- uses time order, or sequence of events
- has transition words to help the reader follow the story

SENTENCE HIGHLIGHT #3

Narrative paragraphs often use time order transitions. The transitions signal the reader as the story moves from one event to the next.

TO SHOW TIME

later	before	an hour earlier
after	as soon as	next
at once	last	first, second, etc.
meanwhile	while	as long as
when	until	at the same time
then	finally	during the morning, day
for a minute	today, tomorrow, last night	

Here are sample sentences showing how time transitions can be used to help the reader follow events.

1. President Olds caught the plane. **Meanwhile**, back at the office, his secretary caught up on the typing.
2. **During** the lunch break, Jake always grabs a sandwich at the coffee shop, **then** heads for the park where he feeds the pigeons.
3. **As soon as** George finishes repairing the flat tire, he will have to remount it.
4. **Finally, after** letting the primer dry thoroughly, use a roller to apply the finish coat.
5. **First of all**, I deposited $175 in the account. **Two days later**, I withdrew $90. **When** my next paycheck arrived, I returned to the bank.

You will have a chance to use these time order transition words in the exercise that follows. Be sure to refer to the list above if you need help.

Exercise C: Transition Words in a Narrative Paragraph

Each group of sentences below represents a sequence of events. By introducing some of the sentences with good transition words (from Sentence Highlight #3) and combining some sentences (from Sentence Highlight #2), turn the sentences into a good narrative paragraph.

1. My sister helped catch a robber.
   She was walking home from work.
   She noticed someone lurking on the corner.
   She saw him take a gun from his pocket.
   The man crossed the street in front of her.
   He walked into the drugstore.
   My sister went to a nearby phone booth.
   She called the police.
   The robber pulled out his gun.
   They arrived in time.
   The man was arrested.

2. I moved to Chicago.
   I started looking for a job.
   I called someone I had known in school.
   He invited me to come for an interview.
   He hired me to do temporary administrative work.
   I found a permanent job somewhere else.
   I quit.

3. Wes fell asleep.
   His cigarette fell from his hand.
   It fell on his newspaper.
   The paper flared quickly.
   The smoke alarm went off.
   His twelve-year-old son burst out of the kitchen.
   He threw the dishpan full of soapy water on the flames.
   They sizzled and went out.
   Wes snored loudly.

4. Mildred married Harold in 1929.
   He lost all his money in the Depression.
   They moved in with her parents to save money.
   Harold didn't find a job until 1937.
   They had two children.
   Harold fell in love with a young cousin, Betsy.
   He and Betsy ran off together in 1938.
   Harold and Betsy are still missing.

MODEL NARRATIVE PARAGRAPHS ARE ON PAGE 94.

Exercise D: Writing Narrative Paragraphs

From the nine topics below, choose <u>two</u> that interest you. If you can, start by writing a topic sentence for each that reflects a narrative purpose. Next, write a narrative paragraph for the two topics chosen. Remember to use a brainstorm list or cluster map. When you are finished, use the checklist on page 77 to make sure your narrative paragraph is a good one.

1. the worst day of my life

2. a very embarrassing moment

3. my first day on the job

4. the argument I had with a co-worker (or boss)

5. my day at the amusement park

6. losing a wallet

7. falling in love

8. moving away from home

9. the most exciting thing I ever did

A MODEL NARRATIVE PARAGRAPH IS ON PAGE 94.

Writing a Descriptive Paragraph

As you know, paragraphs that describe a person, place, object, or event are called **descriptive** paragraphs. The writer creates a vivid picture based on one or more of the five senses. When you write a descriptive paragraph, you will use sensory details that help your reader "see, hear, touch, taste, and smell" what you are describing. The more precisely detailed you make your paragraph, the better the reader will be able to "experience" it.

To make your paragraphs more descriptive, you can do several things: add sensory details, use specific nouns (names of people or things) and verbs (action words), and use precise adjectives (words that describe nouns) and adverbs (words that describe verbs). Making comparisons can also help your reader understand your description better.

When writing a descriptive paragraph, you want to create a mental picture for your reader. You want to describe something with as many important and specific details as you can. Look at the following paragraph and see if you can get a vivid picture of what the writer is describing.

> The fire at 25th and Washington was very big. Smoke came from the windows and rooftop, and flames were everywhere. Fire fighters sprayed water as the crowd gathered to watch. The smell was unbelievably bad, and you could hear yelling from inside the building.

Although you can get some picture of this scene, the writer could do a better job by using more adjectives and adverbs and more specific action words. A better descriptive paragraph of the same scene is given below:

> *The blazing fire at 25th and Washington was completely out of control.* Black and gray smoke billowed out of the smashed windows and sunken rooftop, and bright orange flames leapt from every corner. Charging fire fighters sprayed enormous jet streams of water as a devastated crowd gathered to watch in silence. The harsh and bitter smell from the rising smoke stung the noses of those nearby, and shrill cries of pain and agony echoed from within.

MODEL
Descriptive Paragraph

Notice that, by using more specific language, the writer has given the reader a better, more descriptive picture of the scene. Instead of the common word *big*, the fire is now described as *out of control*. Instead of just saying the smoke *came from* the windows, the writer uses the vivid picture of *billowing*. Throughout the paragraph, adjectives and adverbs are used to appeal to all of the reader's senses—sight, sound, smell, and touch. Not only do these descriptions make a paragraph more interesting, but they also help the readers see what you, the writer, want them to see.

For example, if your purpose in writing is to describe how you felt when your son graduated from high school, you want your reader to really understand what it was like for you. The more specific you can be with your words, the more your reader will be able to "feel" what you felt. Just saying "I was happy" does not really tell the reader much about your feelings. *Happy* is one of those words that is used over and over again in hundreds of situations to mean hundreds of different things. If you want your reader to know how you really felt, use a more specific word, such as *pleased*, *thrilled*, or *triumphant*. These words have different shades of meaning, and all can be used in place of the common term *happy*. In the next two exercises, you'll have a chance to use more descriptive and specific words to improve sentences and paragraphs.

Exercise E: Using Specific Language

The following words in parentheses are frequently overused and are therefore lifeless. When used in sentences, they do not tell the reader a great deal. In the sentences following each overworked word, fill in a more specific and descriptive word. Try to make your reader "see" exactly what you are describing. Of course, there are many ways to fill in each blank.

(walked)

1. As he _____ out of the building, the thief quickly blended in with the crowd.

2. The concerned father quietly _____ into his daughter's room, careful not to wake her.

3. Sheena and Sanford _____ carelessly down the sidewalk, unaware of everything going on around them.

(pretty)

4. Paolo thought Darlene was unbelievably _____, and her warm smile was her best feature.

5. The _____ view from the open window took Tim's breath away.

6. The woman with the long and _____ hair has been seen in countless shampoo ads.

(quickly)

7. Because the supervisor was coming by at two o'clock, the staff had to organize themselves _____.

8. The chimpanzee _____ maneuvered his way up the tree and hid in the leaves.

9. The sprinter reached the finish line _____ and efficiently.

POSSIBLE ANSWERS ARE ON PAGE 94.

Exercise F: Using More Descriptive Language

The following paragraphs use common and lifeless words to describe people, places, events, and feelings. Cross out any words you want to change. Replace weak verbs, adjectives, and adverbs with strong, descriptive ones. You may also add your own words or phrases to help the reader "see" what you are describing. Finally, rewrite your final paragraphs on a separate sheet of paper.

1. The waitress put a big plate of spaghetti in front of Wayne. The red sauce was dripping off the dish, and noodles hung off the sides. The waitress went back into the kitchen and came out with a basket of bread. She looked like the decor in the noisy restaurant; they were both old and tired.

2. The baby sat on the blanket, drooling. She made baby noises and moved her head up and down. Near her on the floor were many toys. She held a rattle.

3. I was unhappy after I got married. I felt I had made a mistake. My wife didn't seem to want to be around me, and we had arguments. I started working a lot so I wouldn't have to go home.

4. The small gray house looked old. However, the porch had many plants on it. The front door was painted. Curtains hung in the windows. The yard was neat. A woman sat knitting in a chair on the porch.

5. The boy was wearing a jacket and jeans. He had a girl with him. She wore high-heeled shoes and a dress and makeup. They went to a party on his motorcycle.

MODEL IMPROVED PARAGRAPHS ARE ON PAGE 95.

Exercise G: Writing a Descriptive Paragraph

Using what you now know about specific and descriptive language, choose <u>one</u> topic below and describe what you want your reader to "see." Be careful <u>not</u> to use tired and lifeless words. Remember to make a brainstorm list or cluster map before you begin writing.

1. what you see outside your bedroom window
2. how you feel when the person closest to you lets you down
3. your least favorite sound or smell
4. the kitchen where your favorite food is being prepared
5. how you feel when you have the flu
6. a busy street

A MODEL DESCRIPTIVE PARAGRAPH IS ON PAGE 95.

Spatial Development

As you have learned, when you write a descriptive paragraph, you want to create a mental picture for your reader. When you are describing something visual, such as a person or a scene, you may want to use **spatial development** in your paragraph. Just as you put thoughts in a time order with a narrative paragraph, you can put thoughts in space order in a descriptive paragraph.

Remember, you want your paragraph to be unified. Putting your descriptive sentences in the order that they might be seen by an observer is one of the best ways to help achieve this unity. For example, if you wanted to describe a person, it would be confusing for the reader if you started with the feet, moved to the nose, then went back to the legs. Wouldn't it make more sense to start at the head and move down or at the feet and move up?

You, as the writer, should pick a place to start the description. You will want to pick a specific point that is often the most important or the most eye-catching detail. From this point, move in a consistent direction through the rest of the scene. There are several possibilities: *top to bottom, bottom to top; right to left, left to right; front to back;* even *clockwise* or *counterclockwise.* What direction does the following paragraph take?

> *My son's kitchen cabinet is so neatly organized.* There are four different kinds of beans on the **top** shelf. On the **next** shelf **beneath** that, there are two kinds of rice and some flour. On the next shelf **below**, there are cans of tomato sauce and three kinds of pasta. The **bottom** shelf is filled mostly with jars of preserves and jam.

MODEL
Spatial Order

Notice how each new detail added was explained in spatial relationship to the other details. The spatial movement was from top to bottom. Notice also how the words in dark print help you to move smoothly and clearly from one detail to the next. These transition and describing words are important in all kinds of paragraphs. To see more of these words and phrases that are useful in descriptive paragraphs, take a look at Sentence Highlight #4.

Comparison/Contrast

Another type of development that can be used effectively for descriptive paragraphs is **comparison/contrast**. Sometimes ideas or details are organized according to their similarities and differences. Pointing out similarities is called *comparison*. Pointing out differences is called *contrast*. This type of paragraph development is very successful because no two people, places, things, or ideas are exactly alike, but they may not be completely different either.

Some paragraphs only compare. They explain only similarities, as in the paragraph below.

> *My two cousins look so much alike you would think they were twins.* **Both** are tall and slender with thick, straight brown hair and soft green eyes. Their short noses and round chins look just the **same**. They even **dress** alike in simple pullover sweaters and comfortable slacks. The most confusing **similarities** are in their walk and gestures. You have to know them well to tell them apart.

MODEL
Comparison

Notice how the similarities are made clear by listing specific details that you can see in your mind's eye. The more specific and complete the details, the clearer the picture or ideas will be.

SENTENCE HIGHLIGHT #4

When writing about spatial relationships, you will want to make it as easy as possible for the reader to follow as you move from place to place. There are many descriptive words and phrases that show how one thing is located in relationship to another. These will help you get a clearer picture across to your reader.

TO SHOW SPACE RELATIONSHIP

at the left, right	in front of
here, there	beyond
west, east, north, south	beneath, under, below
farther on	behind, in back of
nearby, next to	around
on the opposite	inside, in
above, on top of	along the
to the right	in the center
in the foreground	

Here are some examples of how you could use some of these transitions to link two things in space.

1. **On** the wall **opposite** the clock is a huge map of the U.S. and Canada.
2. Paper of different sizes and colors is stored in a cabinet **under** the copy machine.
3. **Across** town, about five miles **west** of here, is the new sports center.
4. **Through** this door is the coffee room, and two doors **down on the left** is the rest room.
5. **Just beyond** the Texaco station, **next to** the Downtown Deli, you'll find the best used furniture store in El Paso.

Make the spatial relationships clear by presenting them in a logical order so that your readers can mentally follow. Otherwise, your readers will become frustrated and hopelessly lost. Instead of a clear picture, they may see something much different from what you want them to see.

Other paragraphs only contrast. They explain only the differences, as in the paragraph below.

> *Although Lynnwood and Ballard are only ten miles apart, they are very different communities.* Lynnwood is a growing suburb of a large city. Ballard, **on the other hand**, is a slowly shrinking, older section of the same city. Lynnwood lies just off a freeway and is dotted with fast food joints, supermarkets, and malls. Ballard has just one main commercial street with a variety of older, smaller shops. Lynnwood has many new apartment buildings and condominiums **while** Ballard has older frame houses. I can't help wondering if the people in Lynnwood and Ballard are **as different as** their surroundings.

MODEL
Contrast

The specific details help you see what the writer is describing. Notice how each difference was explained, first for Lynnwood and then for Ballard. Staying with the same order each time keeps the ideas sorted out.

Some paragraphs explain both similarities and differences, and it doesn't make any difference which comes first. You can start with differences or with similarities. It's your choice.

Transition and describing words help to make the points of similarity and difference easier to spot. Look at Sentence Highlight #5 for transitions and describing words to use in comparison/contrast paragraphs.

SENTENCE HIGHLIGHT #5

In comparison/contrast writing, you will want to use words that tell the reader when you are shifting from similarities to differences or vice versa.

TO SHOW SIMILARITIES

both	a comparable
similarly	and
also	in the same way
in like manner	in common
likewise	as if

Here are some examples of how you could use these words to show similarities between two people, places, objects, or ideas.

1. **Both** Marvin and Wanda are taking a photography class at the YMCA.
2. LaVerne's kitchen is kept in exactly **the same way** her mother's was.
3. Athletes usually have at least three things **in common**: sweat, determination, and competitive spirit.
4. Miami, Florida, is hot and humid in the summer. **Similarly**, Washington, DC, is sticky during June and July.

TO SHOW DIFFERENCES

in contrast	yet
while	however
unlike	whereas
on the other hand	nevertheless
but	in spite of
although	despite the fact that
on the contrary	instead
still	

Here are some sample sentences showing how these words can be used to point out differences.

1. I could go to the bank at lunchtime. **On the other hand**, it will be less crowded after 2:00.
2. **Despite the fact that** Douglas Nancarrow is very well organized, the workers in his department never seem to be.
3. **While** sub-compact cars are less expensive, mid-size cars are more durable.
4. **Unlike** other brands of potato chips, Wilson's claims to use only natural ingredients.

Chapter Checklist

A good narrative paragraph	An effective descriptive paragraph
□ has a topic sentence that reflects the purpose	□ uses strong, specific words to describe
□ uses time order, or sequence of events	□ has connecting words and phrases between sentences that help the reader follow the description
□ has transition words to help the reader follow the story	□ might use spatial development or compare/contrast development
□ uses transitions to help sentences flow	□ lets readers "see" what the writer intended
□ has a good unifying statement at the end	

In the exercise that follows, you will have a chance to brainstorm ideas for descriptive paragraphs. Remember to use the checklist to help you come up with descriptive ideas.

Exercise H: Prewriting for a Descriptive Paragraph

Choose <u>one</u> topic sentence from the list below for your descriptive paragraph. Underline the topic sentence you choose. Brainstorm a list or make a cluster map of details that relate to the topic sentence. Next, select the details that are descriptive and cross out the others.

Topic Sentences:

1. The view from my window is really spectacular.

2. As I walked into the apartment building, I was startled by how much more modern it was than my old building.

3. There is a big difference between riding a bicycle to work and driving a car.

4. The old woman looked as if she'd just come in out of a rainstorm.

5. I was more impressed with this year's car show than I was with last year's.

6. New York City is an exciting place compared to my little town.

7. I'll never forget the expressions on my kids' faces as they opened their Christmas presents.

8. The building across the street is still under construction.

9. Each layer of the dessert looked more delicious that the next.

A MODEL BRAINSTORM LIST IS ON PAGE 96.

Exercise I: Writing a Descriptive Paragraph

Look at your brainstorm list or cluster map from Exercise H above. Now, write a paragraph from it. First, ask yourself whether your paragraph would be best developed using comparison/contrast or spatial development. Look back at the models in this section to help you decide. Refer to Sentence Highlights #4 and #5 for help in using good transition words. Finally, look at the chapter checklist to make sure your descriptive paragraph is complete.

A MODEL DESCRIPTIVE PARAGRAPH IS ON PAGE 96.

Portfolio Activity #2

1. In this portfolio activity, you will **hand in two complete assignments by choosing <u>two</u> paragraphs**. One paragraph must be narrative and the other must be descriptive. Choose paragraphs from your responses to Exercises D, G, and I from Chapter 4.

   If you prefer, you may write a completely new paragraph for either or both of the two paragraph types. For a new narrative piece, write about an episode on a TV show. For a new descriptive paragraph, choose an item in your home and describe it in detail. Remember to use a prewriting method (brainstorming or clustering).

2. Next, **prepare a cover page** for each of your two assignments. Use the model from Portfolio Activity #1.

3. Now, you will **add one more page to your portfolio**. On a new sheet of paper, called the **criteria page**, you will try to develop your own personal system to judge your writing ability. Again, you may use the format below.

In terms of your writing ability, what are your

1. strengths?

   _____

   _____

2. weaknesses?

   _____

   _____

3. goals for improvement?

   _____

   _____

Based on your answers to the questions above, you will make your own checklists. Start with the Chapter Checklist on page 89, and then add your own specific points to remember.

ANSWERS

Exercise A

1. *Descriptive*   The paragraph <u>helps you get a picture</u> in your mind of the difference in appearance between the mother and daughter.

2. *Narrative*   The paragraph <u>tells a story</u> about getting and losing a filling.

3. *Informative*   This paragraph <u>gives you some facts</u> and an explanation of why many teenagers decide to give birth.

4. *Persuasive*   The writer wants <u>to convince you</u> to monitor how tax money is spent.

5. *Descriptive*   The paragraph <u>gives you a picture</u> of both the scene and Leroy's feelings.

6. *Narrative*   You are <u>told a story</u> about what happened when the writer asked Loretta out.

7. *Persuasive*   The writer wants <u>to convince</u> the representative to help her get her check.

Exercise B

Here are some models for you to check your work against. If you're still not sure about your answer, check your topic sentence against the explanations of narrative, descriptive, informative, and persuasive paragraphs on page 69. Then, be sure your topic sentence tells the reader what you want to say about the topic.

1. **Topic:** opening a savings account

   Persuasive topic sentence: Everyone needs to open a savings account at a young age.

   Narrative topic sentence: Let me tell about the time I was ten years old and went in with my father to open my first savings account.

   Informative topic sentence: At First Federal Bank, three different types of savings accounts are available to you.

2. **Topic:** playing the lottery

   Narrative topic sentence: You'll never believe what happened to me last week when I played the lottery.

   Descriptive topic sentence: The faces of people standing in line to buy lottery tickets are always filled with blind hope.

   Persuasive topic sentence: You should buy more than one lottery ticket to improve your chances!

3. **Topic:** financing a child's education

   Informative topic sentence: Parents today are able to finance their children's educations with loans, direct financial aid, and work-study programs.

   Descriptive topic sentence: You should have seen my husband and me the night before those dreadful financial aid forms were due.

Narrative topic sentence: My daughter wanted to go to a private college, so she applied for an academic scholarship at Pacific College.

4. **Topic:** filling out income tax forms

   Descriptive topic sentence: The long income tax form looks pretty complicated.

   Narrative topic sentence: The first year I had to do my own taxes it must have taken me six hours to fill out the short form.

   Informative topic sentence: Most people can choose from among several different kinds of income tax forms.

5. **Topic:** civil rights in your community

   Informative topic sentence: I'd like to explain why our church feels that it should become involved in the issue of civil rights in this community.

   Narrative topic sentence: In the summer of 1964, I was involved in a civil rights demonstration right here in front of this building.

   Persuasive topic sentence: You may think that issues of civil rights are a thing of the past, but I say that's not true here in Cicero.

6. **Topic:** problem with locks on your apartment building or house

   Narrative topic sentence: One day when Laura came home from school, she was unable to work the key in the lock.

   Descriptive topic sentence: The locks look like they are about to fall off the doors.

   Persuasive topic sentence: You must replace the locks on all the apartments in order to ensure the safety of our possessions.

7. **Topic:** quitting school before graduation

   Narrative topic sentence: Because of my mother's illness, I had to quit school to take care of my brothers.

   Informative topic sentence: Every year, several hundred students leave this school without graduating.

   Persuasive topic sentence: If you quit school, you should go to a night high school or GED class.

Exercise C

Here are the sentences made into narrative paragraphs. Yours may not be quite the same. Check to be sure that your transition and combining words make sense and that you have smoothed out all the short choppy sentences.

1. My sister helped catch a robber. **While** she was walking home from work, she noticed someone lurking on the corner. **Then**, she saw him take a gun from his pocket. **Next**, he crossed the street in front of her and walked into the drugstore. **Meanwhile**, my sister went to a nearby phone booth and called the police. The robber pulled out his gun **just as** they arrived, **and finally** the man was arrested.

2. **When** I first moved to Chicago, I started looking for a job. I called someone I had known in school, and **at once** he invited me to come for an interview. He hired me to do temporary administrative work. **As soon as** I found a permanent job somewhere else, I quit.

3. Wes fell asleep. **A minute later**, his cigarette fell from his hand. **Then**, it fell on his newspaper, which flared quickly. **Immediately**, the smoke alarm went off. **At the same time**, his twelve-year-old son burst out of the kitchen **and** threw the dishpan full of soapy water on the flames. They sizzled and went out. **Meanwhile**, Wes snored loudly.

4. Mildred married Harold in 1929. **Soon after**, he lost all his money in the Depression, **so** they moved in with her parents to save money. Harold didn't find a job **until** 1937. **Meanwhile**, they had two children. **Then**, Harold fell in love with a young cousin, Betsy. He and Betsy ran off together in 1938, **and to this day** Harold and Betsy are still missing.

Exercise D

Here is a model paragraph for topic #8, "moving away from home." Even if you chose this topic, your paragraph will probably be very different. Notice that the writer of this paragraph uses sequence of events development and good transition words.

> The day I moved away to Texas my family went a little crazy. I woke up that morning to find my ten-year-old sister tying me to the bedpost with one of my best ties and announcing that she would not let me go. Finally, I freed myself to go downstairs. My mother, who hasn't fixed my breakfast since I was about six, was making me bacon and eggs. Then, my fifteen-year-old sister appeared in an old black dress of my mother's and said she was in mourning for me!

Exercise E

Remember that you may use many different words to replace the dull, lifeless ones. The ones given below are just examples.

1. As he **slithered** out of the building, the thief quickly blended in with the crowd.

2. The concerned father quietly **tiptoed** into his daughter's room, careful not to wake her.

3. Sheena and Stanford **strolled** carelessly down the sidewalk, unaware of everything going on around them.

4. Paolo thought Darlene was unbelievably **attractive**, and her warm smile was her best feature.

5. The **gorgeous** view from the open window took Tim's breath away.

6. The woman with the long and **luxurious** hair has been seen in countless shampoo ads.

7. Because the supervisor was coming by at two o'clock, the staff had to organize themselves **rapidly**.

8. The chimpanzee **speedily** maneuvered his way up the tree and hid in the leaves.

9. The sprinter reached the finish line **swiftly** and efficiently.

Exercise F

Here are the paragraphs rewritten in more specific language. Look at the way you rewrote the paragraphs and see if you have created a vivid, interesting picture for the reader. After looking at these versions, go back to yours and see if you can make them even more specific.

1. The tired waitress plopped a huge platter of spaghetti down in front of Wayne. The tomato sauce slopped over the edge, and pasta drooped over onto the tabletop. The waitress returned briefly to the kitchen and then reappeared with a plastic basket piled with garlic bread. She fit in well with the shabby decor of the chaotic restaurant: old and worn out.

2. The chubby baby plopped on the blanket, drooling enthusiastically. She gurgled and shouted, bobbing her head. Scattered around the room were her rejected blocks, dolls, stuffed animals, and other toys. She joyfully waved her favorite rattle.

3. I was absolutely miserable after I got married. I was positive I had made a terrible mistake. My wife acted as though she couldn't stand the sight of me, and we had terrible fights. I started working night and day to keep myself out of our apartment, which had come to feel like a battlefield.

4. The tiny old gray house drooped and sagged. However, the porch was covered with green and flowering plants. The front door was freshly painted a bright yellow. Clean white curtains hung neatly in the front windows. The small yard was neatly mowed and raked. A woman knitted in a chair on the porch, rocking peacefully.

5. The teenage boy swaggered out in a black leather jacket and tight black jeans. He had a tall black-haired girl on his arm. She was decked out in four-inch spike-heeled shoes, a low-cut black dress, and heavy theatrical makeup. They roared off to a wild party on his Harley-Davidson.

Exercise G

Here is a model descriptive paragraph for topic #2, "how you feel when the person closest to you lets you down." Remember to check your work to make sure your language is as precise and descriptive as the paragraph below.

When my girlfriend forgets to meet me when she is supposed to and then is cold and withdrawn when I try to talk to her, it makes me feel lonely and miserable. Although I'm angry with her, I cannot say so because I'm terrified that she will leave me. This frustration and loneliness makes me feel as if a ton of lead is pounding on my chest.

Exercise H

Below is a sample brainstorm list for a descriptive paragraph about topic #8. Notice that the writer crossed out ideas that were not descriptive.

workmen on roof
piles of bricks all over the ground
no walls yet   ~~project started~~
on the top floors   ~~in March~~

lower part of building
covered by scaffolding
~~I'd like to learn carpentry~~

Exercise I

Here is a model paragraph written from the brainstorm list above, using spatial development. Look over your paragraph to make sure that it creates a clear picture for the reader, that the details are described in a logical order, and that everything you included relates to the topic and is descriptive.

> The building across the street is still under construction. There are workmen walking across the roof, so close to the edge that they practically fall off. Some of the walls on the top two floors aren't in yet. The lower half of the building is encased in scaffolding. At the bottom of the scaffolding are piles of bricks that diminish every day.

5. Paragraphs: Persuading and Informing

Writing a Persuasive Paragraph

Paragraphs that give an opinion and try to convince others to believe or behave in a certain way are called **persuasive** paragraphs. These paragraphs require you to state an opinion and then support it with reasons or facts. Your topic sentence should reflect your purpose by stating your topic and your opinion on it. The supporting sentences should back up your opinion in some way. These sentences can be facts based on some research you have done, or they simply can be facts that you are aware of or incidents from your life. Look at the model below and see how events are used to support a writer's opinion.

> *Sharon, I think you should join Alcoholics Anonymous.* You have been late or absent from work more and more often. Your friend Ted told me that you have begun sneaking drinks at work and acting paranoid around your friends lately. It is obvious that you are not getting along with your family either. AA can give you a new lease on life. I've heard good things about the program. Why don't you talk to your husband about it?

MODEL
Persuasive

In this paragraph, the writer gives several specific reasons that support her topic sentence and her opinion. Most of these reasons are personal incidents that led the writer to believe that Sharon needed help. Sometimes, however, sentences in persuasive paragraphs can be facts and data that support the opinion in the topic sentence.

When you want to express your opinion on an issue, you will want to do so as convincingly and persuasively as possible. You want your reader to respect your opinion and perhaps even change his or her point of view on the matter. To help you be more persuasive in your writing, here are some hints.

STEP 1. STATE YOUR POSITION SIMPLY AND CLEARLY IN THE TOPIC SENTENCE. Suppose your topic is "expanding the church hall to hold more people." To support whether this should or should not be done, you should state your opinion in the first sentence:

Expanding our church hall would be a big mistake.

OR

I do not believe that we should use our funds to expand the church hall.

OR

We need to expand our church hall to hold more people.

OR

I think we should expand our church hall.

All of these topic sentences clearly and forcefully state the opinion of the writer. They would all make good topic sentences to introduce a paragraph. Later, as your writing skills improve, you will learn that you can put these topic sentences elsewhere in a paragraph, but for now the best place is first.

Remember that there is no "right" or "wrong" point of view in persuasive writing. Don't be afraid to say what you think, as long as you can support your opinion with details that support your topic. Your purpose in writing a persuasive paragraph is to make the reader believe or do something. In the next exercise, practice expressing your point of view by thinking about what you want your reader to think or do. Also, practice taking a stand on some topics even if you do not feel strongly about them. You may learn something about yourself while your writing improves!

Exercise A: State Your Opinion

Below you are given several topics. Choose a point of view on each of them and write a strong topic sentence expressing that point of view. To help you decide on your topic sentence, answer the questions for each topic. The example is completed for you.

EXAMPLE: Topic: traveling alone

What do I want my reader to think or do? *to realize that traveling alone can be safe and enjoyable*

Topic sentence: *Although you may not realize it, traveling alone can be both safe and enjoyable.*

1. Topic: gun control

   What do I want my reader to think or do? _____

   _____

   Topic sentence: _____

   _____

2. Topic: your company's wage scale

   What do I want my reader to think or do? _____

   _____

   Topic sentence: _____

   _____

3. Topic: doctor's fees

   What do I want my reader to think or do? _____

   _____

   Topic sentence: _____

   _____

4. Topic: Italian food

   What do I want my reader to think or do? _____

   _____

   Topic sentence: _____

   _____

5. Topic: four-day work or school week

What do I want my reader to think or do? _____

_____

Topic sentence: _____

_____

6. Topic: daytime television

What do I want my reader to think or do? _____

_____

Topic sentence: _____

_____

POSSIBLE ANSWERS ARE ON PAGE 115.

STEP 2. MAKE SURE YOUR SUPPORTING SENTENCES GIVE SPECIFIC REASONS OR FACTS TO BACK UP YOUR OPINION. Once you have stated your opinion in the topic sentence, use the brainstorm technique to help you jot down all the reasons you can think of that will help persuade your reader. As mentioned above, reasons can be researched facts or examples of personal experiences and knowledge. Whatever reasons you choose to support your topic sentence, remember that they must help convince the reader. Below is a possible brainstorm list for one of the topic sentences listed above.

TOPIC SENTENCE: We need to expand our church hall to hold more people.

standing room only now
would be able to attract new members
save money by holding
large functions here
~~grounds need improvement too~~
choir will have room to practice

Notice that the writer has crossed out "grounds need improvement too." Why? Although it might be a true statement, it is not a reason to expand the church hall. In other words, it does not support the topic sentence.

Here is a persuasive paragraph written from this brainstorm list. Notice that the writer's opinion is stated clearly and strongly in the topic sentence and that the following sentences support the stated opinion.

> *We need to expand the church hall to hold more people.* As it is now, there is "standing room only" at all our Sunday services. In addition, with a larger facility, we would probably be able to attract the new membership that we need so badly. Instead of renting space for our larger functions, we could save money by holding them in our own hall. Also, our choir would finally have space to practice—something it has needed for a long time. I believe that if we make these changes now, the future of our church community will be brighter.

MODEL
Persuasive

In the exercise that follows, practice supporting a given topic sentence. You will want to jot down a brainstorm list or cluster map of your reasons before writing the complete paragraph.

Exercise B: Supporting Your Opinion

Choose <u>one</u> of the following topic sentences and underline which of the two positions you are taking. On a separate piece of paper, write a complete paragraph using this as your topic sentence. Make sure that each of your supporting sentences helps to convince the reader of your point of view.

1. I (think/do not think) that the legal voting age should be raised to 21.

2. Belief in Santa Claus (is/is not) healthy for a ten-year-old child.

3. This community (should/should not) spend an additional $7,000 on programs for the elderly.

4. In general, people today are (more/less) interested in keeping America clean and beautiful than they were twenty years ago.

5. Meat and potatoes (are/are not) the healthiest foods to eat.

A MODEL PERSUASIVE PARAGRAPH IS ON PAGE 116.

STEP 3. END YOUR PARAGRAPH WITH A STRONG CONCLUDING SENTENCE. This will help reinforce your point of view in the reader's mind. A concluding sentence can be a simple rewording of your topic sentence. In a persuasive paragraph, it is often effective to tell the reader the consequences of your point of view. For example, in the concluding sentence on the previous page, the writer says that if the church hall is expanded, the church's future will be brighter. Another strong concluding sentence might tell the reader what would happen if the advice is *not* followed:

> I believe that if these changes are not made, our church community will suffer both financial and spiritual losses.

In the next exercise, you will have a chance to practice writing persuasively. As you get ready to write, first remember to state your opinion clearly. There is never any right or wrong point of view in persuasive writing. The most important step is to support your opinion with personal incidents or knowledge and facts. Remember to write a strong and persuasive concluding sentence.

Exercise C: Writing Persuasively

Very often you may find yourself in a situation in which you have to give your opinion on an issue or a statement. This happens in everyday life, in class assignments, and on writing tests. In this exercise, you are given several situations that call for you to give an opinion or to persuade someone to see your point of view. Or, you may be given a situation and question and be asked to write a paragraph of your own in answer to the question.

Choose <u>only one</u> of these situations and write a persuasive paragraph for it. Remember to state your position clearly in the topic sentence, then support this opinion with good reasons. To further emphasize your point of view, make your concluding sentence a strong statement of opinion.

1. Don has just been told that he is being offered an exciting new position with his company. While having a drink with his supervisor after work, Don begins to suspect that he is being chosen ahead of a fellow employee simply because the other employee is of a different nationality.

   Don knows his co-worker's job performance is excellent, but he is also confident in his own abilities. He wants this promotion very badly, but he feels that his supervisor's decision may be unfair. Should Don accept the position?

2. You recently heard that a friend of yours has been borrowing a great deal of money from some dangerous loan sharks. You're afraid for him and his family, and you think that he could get some help from the police if he would just talk to them. However, your friend has been in trouble for a long time and sees no way out.

   Write a paragraph to try to convince this friend that, although it will be difficult, he should start changing his lifestyle.

3. Think of a movie you have seen or a book you have read. Write a paragraph recommending it to someone you do not know very well.

4. Many social scientists called the youth of the 1980s the "me generation," referring to the self-centered attitudes of many of the young people. These social scientists feel that the social consciousness and caring that represented the youth of the 1960s was replaced with the selfishness and greed of the 1980s.

   Do you agree with these social scientists? Do you think the youths of the 1990s are the same as the youths of the 1980s? Be sure you back up your opinion with specific reasons and examples.

5. When two people care very much for each other, both can benefit a great deal from this loving relationship. They can rely on one another and support one another in difficult times. Sometimes, however, a person may begin to lean too heavily on another. He may lose his own sense of self-worth and feel that he is not a whole person without the other. The relationship becomes a burden to one person and a danger to the other.

   Why does this problem sometimes occur, and what should you do to avoid this problem in a relationship? Be sure to support your explanation with clear examples and reasons.

6. Your best friend is about to spend a lot of money on something you know is not worth it. It could be a car, jewelry, an apartment— anything you know something about.

   Write a paragraph telling this friend why he shouldn't waste his money. Be sure to give specific facts and reasons to support your opinion.

A MODEL PERSUASIVE PARAGRAPH IS ON PAGE 116.

Order of Importance

Order of importance is an effective way to organize the reasons and supporting evidence in persuasive paragraphs. Since you will most likely have several reasons for the opinion stated in your topic sentence, you'll have to decide what order to put them in. For example, if you're writing a letter of complaint about a product and want to convince a company that you deserve a full refund, you should probably put the most important point up front. Tell the reader what is wrong in the first sentence! Get your point across clearly while you have the attention of your reader.

MODEL
Order of Importance

> *I am returning this set of ballpoint pens to your company for several reasons.* Most important, the color ink in each of them is so pale that it can hardly be seen on white paper! Secondly, although your advertisement said that they were made of sturdy plastic, they seem flimsy and cheap to me. In addition, they arrived two weeks late for my father's birthday, and they were supposed to be a gift to him.

Some writers reverse the order and save their most important reason for the end of the paragraph. Here is a model of the same paragraph using the reverse order.

MODEL
Order of Importance

> *I am returning this set of ballpoint pens to your company for several reasons.* The least important reason is that they arrived two weeks late for my father's birthday, and they were supposed to be a gift to him. To top it off, they seem flimsy and cheap to me even though your advertisement said they were made of sturdy plastic. But most of all, the color ink in each of them is so pale that it can hardly be seen on white paper!

No matter which way you choose to write your persuasive paragraph, Sentence Highlight #6 will help you make your reasons clear to the reader.

SENTENCE HIGHLIGHT #6

Paragraphs organized according to order of importance use transition and describing words to show relative importance. Some examples are *more important, less significant, highly critical, first priority,* and *most influential.* Other kinds of transitions used in persuasive paragraphs help the reader follow your line of thought. Some examples are *as a result, furthermore, however, similarly, for example,* and *finally.*

TO SHOW IMPORTANCE

first, second priority	minor
more, most serious	primary, secondary
less, least, not important	foremost
mildly	extremely
slightly	quite
extraordinary influence	very
insignificant	small difference
great	worse, worst
better, best	most of all

Here are some examples of sentences using transition words and describing words to show order of importance.

1. The **least** valid reason to get married, in my opinion, is to have children.
2. My **primary** concern is whether or not there are opportunities to move up in this company.
3. **Slightly more important** is the effect of secondhand smoke on nonsmokers.
4. Safety and convenience are important, but **most of all** we must convince the customer of our product's high quality.

Of course, you can use methods other than order of importance when writing a persuasive paragraph. For example, you may want to use the comparison/contrast development that you learned in Chapter 4. In this case, you could compare what would happen if the reader followed your advice to what would occur if he or she did not. Another method of development, cause and effect, will be discussed later in this chapter, and this method also may be used in persuasive writing. Remember that no matter what method of development you choose for your paragraph, you want to do whatever you can to persuade the reader.

A good persuasive paragraph
- states an opinion clearly in the topic sentence
- supports the opinion with good reasons, accurate facts, and personal experiences
- uses transition and describing words between sentences to help the reader understand importance
- has a strong concluding sentence

Exercise D: Writing a Persuasive Paragraph

Choose only one topic from the list below and write a persuasive paragraph based on it. Use order of importance development in your paragraph, and look back at the models in this chapter if you need help. Also, refer to the checklist above to help you write as persuasively as possible.

1. abortion
2. dieting
3. living together vs. getting married
4. Michael Jackson
5. the minimum wage
6. police brutality
7. American-made vs. foreign automobiles
8. women in the armed forces
9. the salaries of sports stars

A MODEL PERSUASIVE PARAGRAPH IS ON PAGE 116.

Writing an Informative Paragraph

The purpose of an **informative** paragraph is to explain something to the readers or inform them of something that they may not know. Paragraphs that inform use factual details that can be checked or measured. They do *not* state opinions as persuasive paragraphs do.

Informative paragraphs answer questions such as *who, what, where, when, why,* and *how.* They provide knowledge about certain topics and make difficult things easier to understand. You can find many examples of informative writing just by opening up a newspaper or magazine. Except for advertisements and editorials, most of the writing you find there is called informative.

As you go through this section, notice how the topic sentences in informative paragraphs identify the topic. The topic sentence indicates the main idea or the kinds of information the paragraph will explain. The next exercise will give you an idea of the elements of an informative paragraph.

Exercise E: Elements of an Informative Paragraph

Read the informative paragraphs below. In the space beside the question words *who, what, where, when, why,* and *how,* give the information contained in the paragraph. Some of the question words will have several responses, and some will have none. If a paragraph does not directly state an answer to one of the question words, write "does not directly state" in the space provided. Part of the first one has been done for you.

1. Despite generally poor weather that spring, recreational vehicle sales in the U.S. rose 25.3% during the first three months of the year. March sales were the best in nearly six years. Executives said that business got a lift from "baby boomers" who now have children of their own and want an inexpensive means of travel. In fact, a recent University of Michigan study indicated that 40% of households surveyed planned to buy or use a recreational vehicle over the next three years.

Who *executives*   What *recreational vehicles*

When   Where

Why   How

2. In the United States, the first Monday in September is called Labor Day. It is a holiday set aside to honor the workers of the country. Labor Day is not a very old holiday, dating back only to 1882. Many stores and most banks are closed on Labor Day, as well as some offices and factories. Mail carriers do not make deliveries. It is a holiday for all but some workers such as police officers and fire fighters, whose work must go on. But most people celebrate Labor Day by not laboring at all!

Who   What

When   Where

Why   How

3. The chairperson of the Citizen's Transportation Improvement Group today announced a new plan. The plan is to raise funds for the repairing of the town's bike paths and sidewalks. The fund drive is scheduled to begin September 9 and to continue until enough improvements are made. The chairperson hopes that improving these paths and sidewalks will urge more citizens to choose these methods of transportation. In this way, the chairperson hopes to relieve some of the overcrowding on the town bus system.

Who   What

When   Where

Why   How

4. Birth rates in most of the Third World—particularly in its poorest and most unstable regions—are as high as ever. Within the next century, India's population could climb from 675 million to more than 1.6 billion, Nigeria's from 85 million to more than 500 million, and El Salvador's from 5 million to more than 15 million. Worldwide, that could add up to a total of 11 billion before population growth levels off.

Who   What

When   Where

Why   How

ANSWERS ARE ON PAGE 117.

Sequence of Events

Informative paragraphs often give directions or explain how to do something. In such cases, time order, or **sequence of events**, is usually used. As you recall, we talked about sequence of events in Chapter 4. Explaining the steps in the order in which they will be performed makes them easiest for your reader to understand and remember. Again, notice how transition words and phrases are used to help the reader follow directions.

> *Changing a flat tire is quite simple if you follow these steps.* **First**, be sure the emergency brake is on, the car is in gear, and another tire is blocked to prevent rolling. **Second**, take the hubcap off and loosen the nuts. **Third**, jack up the car and take off the nuts and store them in the hubcap. **Next**, put the spare tire on and tighten the nuts only until snug. Let down the jack and finish tightening the nuts. **Finally**, put the hubcap back on and put the jack and flat tire away.

MODEL
**Informative
(Sequence
of
Events)**

In the next exercise, you will have a chance to try writing an informative paragraph with sequence of events development. Remember to use the model above if you need help. Also, be careful not to leave out any important steps.

Exercise F: Writing Directions

Choose one of the topics below, and in one paragraph explain how to perform the task. Use sequence of events to develop your paragraph so that the reader can easily follow your directions.

1. making a cake from a mix

2. walking from your home to the grocery store

3. changing the oil in a car

4. filling out a job application

5. choosing a good stereo system

6. getting from work to your favorite restaurant

7. putting a small child to bed

A MODEL INFORMATIVE PARAGRAPH IS ON PAGE 117.

Cause/Effect

Another useful way to organize ideas in an informative paragraph is in **cause-and-effect** order. Cause is what makes something happen or why something is true. Effect is what happens as a result.

Some paragraphs explain only causes, as shown in the model below. Read it through once. Then, on a separate piece of paper, see if you can list the reasons (or causes) that helped Janie win the race.

MODEL
Causes

Several things helped Janie Bishop win last week's marathon. First, she experimented and found the very best running shoes for her. Second, she's built just right for running. She's lean and long-legged, without an ounce of extra fat. Third, she started training by running home from work and then increased her distance according to a careful schedule. In addition, Janie has personal qualities that help: self-discipline and determination. She truly wants to reach her full potential.

Other paragraphs explain only effects. Again, read the model below, then see if you can list all of the effects of the lottery office announcement.

MODEL
Effects

The lottery office announced that the jackpot for this week's grand drawing had risen to a record $19 million, and the effects of this announcement have been widespread. Lines to purchase still more of the weekly drawing tickets are longer than ever before, and grocery store and shop owners are running out of tickets at an unbelievable rate. The owners also say that they are selling more products and making bigger profits due to the increase in customers passing through their stores. One sure result of the lottery office announcement is that the jackpot will grow even larger.

Some paragraphs explain both causes and effects. Read the model paragraph below, then look at the chart that takes you through the causes and effects the writer has included.

MODEL
Cause and Effect

Sasha Stewart enjoys staying fit and keeping her weight under control. But last year, because of extra eating and a decrease in physical activity, she gained fifteen pounds. So, in January, she decided to try a new diet and exercise program. Her goal was to be her usual trim self by summer. Although it took five months, she managed to lose the fifteen pounds by June.

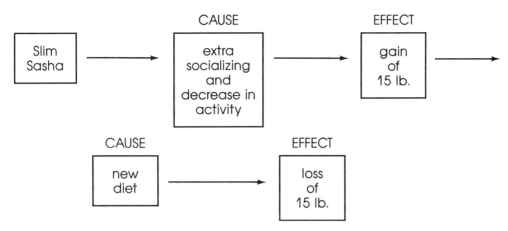

The paragraph and chart above explain the cause-effect chain reaction of Sasha's increased weight. To introduce a cause or an effect or to indicate a shift from one to the other, cause-and-effect paragraphs use transitions such as *because, therefore,* and *consequently.* See Sentence Highlight #7 for more transitions that indicate cause-and-effect relationships. Meanwhile, practice recognizing causes and effects in the next exercise.

Exercise G: Causes and Effects

For each of the following items, decide what some of the causes and effects might be. Write them in the blanks provided. Part of the first one has been done to help you.

Causes		Effects
1. *being nervous*	smoking a lot	*smell like smoke*
2. _____	breaking up with a boy/girlfriend	_____
3. _____	getting fired	_____
4. _____	getting a raise	_____
5. _____	being late for an appointment	_____

POSSIBLE ANSWERS ARE ON PAGE 118.

SENTENCE HIGHLIGHT #7

Informative paragraphs developed with causes and effects use transitions and conjunctions to signal shifts from causes to effects.

TO SHOW CAUSES AND EFFECTS

because	thus	since	unless
so that	for this reason	in order to	so
as a result	it follows that	therefore	consequently

Here are some sample sentences showing cause and effect.

1. **Because** it hasn't rained in over two weeks, the grass is turning brown.
2. **Unless** you make a payment within the week, we'll have to repossess your car.
3. **If** you learn to use a welder, **then** you can save money by making your own repairs on your steel boat.
4. **Once** you've won your case in small claims court, **it follows that** the landlord will return your deposit.
5. **As a result** of the accident, Charles McDade had to have eight stitches in his foot.

Chapter Checklist

A good persuasive paragraph	A good informative paragraph
☐ states an opinion clearly in the topic sentence	☐ directly states the topic in the topic sentence
☐ supports the opinion with good reasons, accurate facts, or personal experiences	☐ presents facts, not opinions
☐ uses transition and describing words between sentences to help the reader understand importance	☐ gives precise instruction or information in a clear order
☐ ends with a strong opinion in the closing sentence	☐ uses transition words to indicate a continuation or change in ideas

Exercise H: Writing Informative Paragraphs

Six topics are listed here. Choose <u>only one</u> and write an informative paragraph using cause or effect or order of importance development. Remember to use Sentence Highlight #7 and the Chapter Checklist to help you. You may want to use a brainstorm list, cluster map, or cause or effect chain.

1. explain how to get from one city to another

2. give information about a decision to rearrange the factory floor

3. inform someone about how the new seat-belt law will affect him or her

4. inform someone about a particular sport

5. tell someone how to play the lottery in your state

6. give information about a subject you know a lot about

A MODEL INFORMATIVE PARAGRAPH IS ON PAGE 118.

Portfolio Activity #3

1. In this activity, you will once again **turn in <u>two</u> complete assignments**. One paragraph will be persuasive and the other will be informative. Choose paragraphs from your responses to Exercises B, C, D, and H from Chapter 5. If you prefer, you may write a completely new paragraph for either or both of the paragraph types.

    For a new persuasive piece, think of a common phrase you hear people say, such as "better late than never" or "too many cooks spoil the broth." Then, decide if you agree or disagree with the phrase, and try to convince your readers of your opinion. Remember to support your opinion with specific reasons or examples.

    For a new informative piece, imagine that it is election time in your city. Your friend is not sure whom to vote for. You do not want to tell your friend which candidate to vote for. Instead, you decide to explain the current issues that are being debated. You hope that if you explain the issues, your friend will be able to find a candidate that best represents his or her feelings about these issues. Remember to use a prewriting method before you begin writing your new paragraph.

2. Next, **prepare a cover page** for each of your two paragraphs. Use the model from Portfolio Activity #1 on page 64.

3. Then, **prepare a criteria page** using the format from Portfolio Activity #2 on page 91. This time, use the checklists for persuasive and informative paragraphs found on page 113 in order to create your personal checklists.

4. When you have gathered together all your material for both paragraphs, **turn everything in to your instructor**.

ANSWERS

Exercise A

These responses and topic sentences are examples of some you may have come up with. Remember that they are not the only correct ones. Check to make sure your topic sentence clearly states your topic and your opinion on that topic.

1. **Topic:** gun control

   What do I want my reader to think or do? to vote against it because it is an unfair restriction on our right to defend ourselves

   Topic sentence: Gun control is an unfair restriction on our rights, and we should all vote against it

2. **Topic:** my company's wage scale

   What do I want my reader to think or do? to see that it should be changed so that the longer you stay with the company, the larger your bonus would be

   Topic sentence: Our company's wage scale should be changed so that those who are with the company longer will get larger bonuses.

3. **Topic:** doctor's fees

   What do I want my reader to think or do? to understand that doctors earn every cent they make

   Topic sentence: Although it is true that many doctors make a great deal of money, I believe they work hard for it and deserve it.

4. **Topic:** Italian food

   What do I want my reader to think or do? to try Italian food

   Topic sentence: You should really give Italian food a try because it tastes great and is very good for you.

5. **Topic:** four-day work or school week

   What do I want my reader to think or do? to realize that 5 days out of 7 is too much time to spend working

   Topic sentence: The five-day work week should be changed to a four-day work week because five days is too great a part of the week to work.

6. **Topic:** daytime television

   What do I want my reader to think or do? to see that it is much more exciting than prime time

   Topic sentence: Daytime TV is more exciting than prime time because the characters are more true to life, and the situations are more believable.

Exercise B

Here is a model paragraph based on #4. Check your own paragraph to see that all sentences support the statement you made in the topic sentence. Do you convince the reader of your point of view? Have someone else read your paper and let you know.

> In general, people are more interested in keeping America clean and beautiful than they were twenty years ago. This is certainly easy to see by just looking around you in parks and other public places. There is very little litter to be seen. Also, in the past several years, the government has set up strict penalties and fines for people caught littering or in any way abusing the environment. Twenty years ago, there were no laws against dumping your trash anywhere you wanted. I think people are realizing that it is their responsibility to keep their world clean.

Exercise C

Below is a model paragraph based on #5. Remember that you may have a completely different point of view and still have written a good paragraph. Check your work to make sure you (1) stated your opinion clearly in the topic sentence, (2) supported your position with facts and experiences, and (3) ended your paragraph with a strong concluding statement.

> A relationship in which one person is too dependent on another happens because one person lacks the self-confidence to be his or her own person. When this person finds someone who loves him and respects him as a person, he will sometimes isolate himself from everyone else. This is how he becomes a burden. To avoid having this happen in a relationship, people should believe in themselves. The saying that you have to love yourself before you can love another is very true in this situation.

Exercise D

Here is a model persuasive paragraph for #3 using order of importance development. Notice that the opinion of the writer is clear from the topic sentence. This opinion is backed up with personal experiences and facts, and the concluding sentence restates the writer's point of view.

> Living together is better than getting married in many respects. First of all, you don't need any piece of paper to do it. You won't have to go to city hall or spend a lot of money on a big wedding. Secondly, you get all of the good things that go with being married without the rotten things. You can still be close to someone and spend all your time with him or her, but you don't necessarily HAVE to do it! But most importantly, it is a lot easier to stop living together than it is to get a divorce. All in all, I think living together has more advantages than being married.

Exercise E

1. **Who**   executives
      baby boomers

   When   first three months of 1984
         March
         next three years

   Why   inexpensive travel

   What   recreational vehicle sales
         University of Michigan study

   Where   United States

   How   does not directly state

2. **Who**   workers

   When   first Monday in September
         back to 1882

   Why   to honor workers

   What   Labor Day

   Where   United States

   How   by closing stores and banks and
         not working

3. **Who**   chairperson of CTIG

   When   today
         September 9

   Why   so citizens will choose this
         method of transportation

   What   plan to raise funds for repairing
         paths and walks

   Where   town

   How   does not directly state

4. **Who**   does not directly state

   When   within next century

   Why   does not directly state

   What   birth rates

   Where   Third World

   How   does not directly state

Exercise F

Here is an informative paragraph based on #7 using sequence of events
development. Check your paragraph to see if you used good transitions to help
your reader follow your directions.

> To put a small child to bed, you must remember to do several
> things. First, put the child in pajamas and have her brush her teeth.
> You should watch to make sure she does it correctly. Next, ask her if
> she needs to use the bathroom before she goes to sleep. Third, put
> the child in bed and read a short bedtime story. Finally, tuck her
> under the covers, turn out the light, and leave the door open a
> crack.

Exercise G

Remember that there are many causes and effects for the items below. These are just examples of some you may have thought of.

Causes		Effects
1. being nervous enjoying taste	**smoking a lot**	smelling like smoke getting cancer
2. finding out she's/he's cheating feeling tied down	**breaking up with boy/girlfriend**	being depressed dating a lot
3. being late too much unjustly accused of stealing	**getting fired**	collecting unemployment filing suit against employer
4. working a lot of overtime getting a promotion	**getting a raise**	buying a new car deciding to stay with company
5. losing car keys given incorrect address	**being late for an appointment**	refused interview rescheduled interview

Exercise H

Here is a model informative paragraph based on #2 using cause-effect development. Use this and the Chapter Checklist to review your own work.

> On August 10 of this year, the management of the factory decided to rearrange the machinery equipment on our floor, and the effects were disastrous. The management did not consult with those who actually operate the equipment. They were therefore unaware of the difficulties the switch created. The men and women who have learned an efficient way to do their work now have to completely readjust to an awkward method. The drill machines have been placed too close to the cutting equipment, and this makes it dangerous for workers to move about freely to do their work. The decision to change the system is angering workers and creating a lot of resentment toward management.

6. Editing Your Work

What Is Editing?

You should now be able to express yourself in well-organized paragraphs. You have learned to put your ideas on paper in a way that helps the reader understand you. The last step in the writing process is called **editing**. Editing, or correcting, your writing also helps the reader understand you better.

Think of how hard it would be for someone to understand what you meant if you didn't use complete sentences, if your spelling were poor, or if you left lots of grammar errors in your paragraph. Writers and teachers don't insist on correct grammar just because it's right. Correcting these mistakes in your writing helps you get your ideas across clearly to your reader.

The best way to edit your work is to take a different-color pen or pencil and actually correct mistakes right on your paper. Don't try to rewrite the paragraph while you fix your mistakes because you may miss some. Just neatly cross out what you want to change and write it correctly in the margin or above it. It will be easy to do this if you write on every other line.

On the next page is a sample of a paragraph that has been edited. Notice how the writer wrote on every other line and left plenty of room to correct mistakes.

Dear Mr. Craig,
Would you please arrange to let my
daughter, Charrise Dalton, out of ~~School~~ *s*
at 12:30 on ~~Thursday~~*? She has a*
appointment
doctor's ~~appointmint~~*. Thank you.*
~~We~~ *will see you on Parents' Day.*
Terry Dalton

In this chapter you will find hints on improving your writing to help your reader. The chapter does not cover every single rule you need for correct writing, but it does give some information on errors that writers frequently make. Go through this chapter and do the exercises. Also, use what you have learned from the Sentence Highlights in this book. If you do these two things, you should be able to edit your work so that your reader will have no problem understanding you.

Is Your Punctuation Correct?

End Punctuation

All sentences in your paragraph should end with either a **period**, a **question mark**, or an **exclamation point**. Check your punctuation and make sure all your sentences are complete. Go back to Sentence Highlight #1 on page 23 and review the difference between a sentence and a fragment.

If you are sure you have written a complete sentence, choose one of the following end punctuation marks:

1. If your sentence is a statement, use a period.
   The new laws are important to all of you.

2. If your sentence is a question, use a question mark.
   Do you really believe we can help?

3. If your sentence shows surprise or lots of emotion, use an exclamation point.
   The members of this organization must unite!

   (Be careful to use the exclamation point only where it is truly needed to get your point across. Using it too much ruins its effect.)

The Comma

You have already seen how a comma is used in combining sentences (Sentence Highlight #2). To refresh your memory:

STEP 1. USE A COMMA BEFORE AND, BUT, OR, FOR, NOR, SO, AND YET WHEN THEY ARE USED TO JOIN TWO SENTENCES. Be sure these conjunctions are joining two complete sentences, not just subjects or predicates.

> Kevin decided to go to Pat's Cafe on Friday.
> Kathryn wanted to go with him.

> BECOMES

> Kevin decided to go to Pat's Cafe on Friday, **and** Kathryn wanted to go with him.

STEP 2. USE A COMMA WHEN A DEPENDENT CLAUSE COMES FIRST IN A SENTENCE. As you'll remember from Sentence Highlight #2, words like *because, although, when, before, unless,* and *as soon as* start dependent clauses. See Sentence Highlight #2 on page 57 for a complete list of this type of conjunction.

When the dependent clause comes before the main part of the sentence, use a comma to separate the two clauses.

> When Cedric is hired, our office will be well staffed.

When the clause beginning with one of the above conjunctions comes last in a sentence, do not use a comma to separate the clauses.

> Our office will be well staffed when Cedric is hired.

STEP 3. USE COMMAS TO SEPARATE ITEMS IN A SERIES. When you are listing more than two items in a series, you should put a comma after each one.

> The maintenance people in our building spent all day painting, scrubbing, and redecorating.

Doing this will help your reader see that you are emphasizing different items. Remember, be sure there are at least three items in your list if you are using commas. Two items joined with *and* or *or* do not need a comma.

> The maintenance people in our building spent all day painting and scrubbing.

STEP 4. USE A COMMA AFTER A GREETING IN AN INFORMAL LETTER AND WITH A DIRECT ADDRESS. The **greeting** of a letter is the introductory part, where you say "Dear Mr. Vangeleo" or "Dear Aunt Francine," before you get to the main point of your letter.

Direct address is when, in writing, you speak to someone in particular. You use a comma following a name that introduces a sentence. For example:

> Mercedes, you will have to come home earlier than this.

If the name of the person being addressed is in the middle of the sentence, a comma should be placed before and after the name.

> I have been told, Congressman Rubin, that you may be able to help me.

If the name of the person being addressed comes at the end of the sentence, just put a comma before it.

> The papers should be signed by noon, Mrs. Ledro.

STEP 5. DON'T USE A COMMA UNLESS YOU KNOW YOU NEED ONE. Writers generally make more mistakes by putting in unnecessary commas than by leaving them out. Before you use a comma, ask yourself why you need one. If you can't think of a rule that says you need the comma, leave it out.

Is Your Capitalization Correct?

You already know that the first word of a sentence must be capitalized. This helps your reader realize that a new sentence is beginning.

Other words in your paragraph may have to be capitalized as well, depending on how you use them. The hints below should help you, but remember that they do not give all capitalization rules.

Proper Nouns

Proper nouns are things like people's names (first and last) and names of cities, states, countries, and other specific places. Proper nouns are always capitalized.

General vs. Specific

Knowing the difference between *general* and *specific* can help you capitalize correctly. Unless you are identifying a specific person, place, or thing, do not capitalize the word.

This rule can get confusing because a word might be capitalized in one sentence but not have a capital in the next sentence. Why? The reason is that the word may be used in two different ways. For example:

> I wrote to **Senator** Smythe today to tell him our concerns.
> Because he is a **senator**, he may be able to help us.

The first time the word *senator* is used, the writer is using it as a specific person's name. *Senator* is part of *Smythe's* title. The second time, the word *senator* does not specifically name a person, place, or thing, but rather the word is used as a general term.

Writers make most of their capitalization errors by capitalizing words they shouldn't. Before you use a capital letter, ask yourself if you are giving the specific name of someone or something. If you are not, chances are you do not need the capital letter.

Before you do the next exercise, look at the following models. See if you can tell why some dark type words are capitalized and some are not.

> The Rocky **Mountains** are the most beautiful **mountains** on earth.
> If you travel **west** on Route 91, you should come to **West** Haven.
> Kathleen's **doctor's** name is **Doctor** Munsat.
> The **Fish** Hut has the best fried **fish** in all of Denver.
> The **company** I am applying to is called Cullen **Company**.

Exercise A: Editing for Punctuation and Capitalization

This exercise has three steps. First, recopy the paragraph below onto another sheet of paper. Be sure to write on every other line. The second step is to edit the paragraph. Correct all punctuation and capitalization errors, keeping in mind what was discussed above and what you learned in the Sentence Highlights. Remember that an error can be an unnecessary comma or capital letter as well as a missing one.

The third step of this exercise is to go back and choose a paragraph that you wrote in Chapter 4 or 5. Now edit that paragraph, remembering to watch for capitalization and punctuation errors.

My Sister suggested, that I write to you to ask about any open positions at your Company. I am an experienced stockroom attendant and my previous Employer will recommend me highly. My duties at Tyson's incorporated included filling orders stocking shelves and getting supplies. Although I have never worked at a place like Pitcom company I believe I can learn quickly. Is it possible for me to come in and discuss this matter Ms. Lee.

THE EDITED VERSION OF THIS PARAGRAPH IS ON PAGE 129.

Did You Check Your Spelling?

There is not enough room here to discuss every spelling rule. Here are some hints, though, to help you check your work.

STEP 1. USE A DICTIONARY FOR WORDS THAT YOU ARE NOT USED TO SPELLING. Although it will take extra time, it is a good idea to look up words that you are not completely sure about. Although you do not know the exact spelling of a word, you will most likely have an idea of the first couple letters. For example, if you did not know how to spell "fragile," you could start by looking under "fr" in the dictionary. Keep guessing at the following letters until you find the word you are looking for. The guide words at the top of the dictionary page will help you. This "trial and error" approach to spelling may take extra time, but your reader will appreciate the effort! Try to keep a dictionary on hand whenever you write.

STEP 2. BEWARE OF WORDS THAT SOUND ALIKE BUT HAVE DIFFERENT SPELLINGS AND MEANINGS. Writers often make the mistake of using *their* instead of *they're* or *there*, *to* or *two* instead of *too*, etc. Most of these mistakes are made when the writer is in a hurry. Try to keep these tricky spellings in mind when you are editing your work. Below is a list of some of these words with their correct uses.

their	pronoun showing possession, as in "their books"
there	adverb telling place
they're	contraction meaning "they are"
to	preposition, as in "to the supermarket"
two	number
too	meaning "also"
its	pronoun meaning "of it"
it's	contraction meaning "it is"
here	adverb telling place
hear	listen

Do You Have Any Run-on Sentences?

Run-on sentences are actually two or more sentences that run together without punctuation. For example:

> We have looked into your program it seems to offer exactly what we are looking for.

The above group of words is actually two complete thoughts. It is not correct because the two thoughts are not separated by proper punctuation.

If you come across a run-on in your work, you can edit it in several ways. Here are two easy ideas:

STEP 1. PUT A PERIOD AFTER THE FIRST COMPLETE THOUGHT AND START THE SECOND WITH A CAPITAL LETTER. In this way, you are making two complete sentences.

> We have looked into your program. It seems to offer exactly what we are looking for.

STEP 2. PUT A COMMA AND A CONJUNCTION AFTER THE FIRST COMPLETE THOUGHT. You will still have one sentence, but it is no longer a run-on. It has a conjunction and correct punctuation.

> We have looked into your program, and it seems to offer exactly what we are looking for.

Remember that a comma alone will <u>not</u> fix a run-on:

> Jack's favorite sport was basketball, he also loved baseball.

You must include a conjunction as well:

> Jack's favorite sport was basketball, **but** he also loved baseball.

Are All Your Sentences Complete?

Since fragments are a common problem for many new writers, it doesn't hurt to check this one more time. Fragments are often hard to pick out in paragraphs because they seem to make sense when read with the sentences around them.

To get around this problem, read each sentence in your paragraph as if it stood on its own. Does it have a subject and a predicate? More important, does it express a complete thought?

Look at the short paragraph below and see if you can pick out the fragment.

> The manager called the customer into her office. Because there was a problem with her check. The customer cleared up the problem easily with a driver's license.

If you read these sentences in paragraph form, they all seem to make sense. If you read each sentence on its own, however, you should be able to spot the fragment. The group of words beginning with the subordinating word *because* is not a sentence. Why not? It does not express a complete thought on its own. If you combine this fragment with the first sentence, you will have a good sentence and a complete thought.

> The manager called the customer into her office because there was a problem with her check.

So, when you are editing your paragraph, be on the lookout for sentences beginning with words like *because, although, since, so that,* and other subordinating words. Make sure the sentence can stand on its own—without the other sentences of the paragraph.

Exercise B: Editing for Run-ons and Fragments

This exercise has two steps. First, edit the paragraph below. You may want to recopy it first onto every other line. It contains run-ons and fragments, as well as one spelling error. The second step is to choose another paragraph you wrote in Chapter 4 or 5. Edit your work, being especially careful about run-ons and fragments.

> Ms. Fargo, my wife and I would like you to watch out for our son, José. He is on special medicine for a leg injury he may have some side effects. Please call us immediately if he seems strange. So that we can call his doctor. If we are not home, José's grandparents are usually in there home at 555-3373.

THE EDITED VERSION OF THIS PARAGRAPH IS ON PAGES 129 AND 130.

Exercise C: More Editing

The paragraphs below have several errors. Edit each of them, keeping in mind what you learned in this chapter and what you learned from the Sentence Highlights in this book. You may also use a dictionary if some of the words are not familiar to you.

1.   My experience as a clerk typist at a large computer Business has helped me develop several important skills. I have learned typing filing and some data processing. Which would be helpful in many new positions. Since I have had too years of secratariel school I also have learned to be professional, at all times on the job. If I come to work at ford motor company, I beleive I would do very well at the duties required. When can I come in for an interview.

2.   My church group has asked me to write a memo explaining what functions we are planning for this summer? I will start off, by saying that all members should have they're ideas ready by April 1. If they want these ideas to be considered by the group. We will come up with a final list by May 1 it will be approved by the group by May 15. Let's get thinking! So that this summer will be a great one!

EDITED VERSIONS OF THESE PARAGRAPHS ARE ON PAGES 130 AND 131.

Portfolio Activity #4

1. Now that you have learned how to edit your paragraphs, you can **edit your own portfolio assignments**. At this time, you should have the following five paragraphs in your portfolio: (1) one selected from Chapter 3, (2) narrative, (3) descriptive, (4) persuasive, and (5) informative.

   Take the time now to edit all five of them. You may want to use a different-color pen or pencil. Remember to check for mistakes in spelling, punctuation, and capitalization. Also, make sure you don't have any run-on sentences or sentence fragments. During the editing process, feel free to change a thought or rewrite a sentence. Remember, writing is a process, and you are in charge. This editing process will be easier if you have written on every other line.

2. You can edit your **cover page** and **criteria page**, too. Check to make sure your sentences are complete and that your spelling, punctuation, and capitalization are all correct.

3. At this point, you should **add the following questions to your cover pages and answer them**.

   1. What did you check most to perfect your paper: spelling, punctuation, or capitalization?
   2. Did your ideas about the topic change while you were working on your paragraph?
   3. What part of the paragraph gave you the most trouble?

4. After you finish editing, think about your paragraphs and the changes you've made. Did you discover some writing **strengths** you did not know you had? Did you find any **weaknesses** that were a surprise? Add new findings such as these to your criteria pages.

ANSWERS

Check your work against the edited paragraphs below. The symbol ∧ is a common editing mark meaning "insert here." Therefore, the mark ⌄ means "insert a comma," and ∧ means "insert a period."

Exercise A

My ~~Sister~~ suggested that I write to you to ask about any open positions at your ~~Company~~. I am an experienced stockroom attendant, and my previous ~~Employer~~ will recommend me highly. My duties at Tyson's ~~incorporated~~ included filling orders, stocking shelves, and getting supplies. Although I have never worked at a place like Pitcom ~~Company~~, I believe I can learn quickly. Is it possible for me to come in and discuss this matter, Ms. Lee?

Exercise B

Ms. Fargo, my wife and I would like you to watch out for our son,

José. He is on special medicine for a leg injury; ~~he~~ He may have some side effects. Please call us immediately if he seems strange, ~~So~~ So that we can call his doctor. If we are not home, José's grandparents are usually in ~~there~~ their home at 555-3373.

Exercise C

1. My experience as a clerk typist at a large computer Business has helped me develop several important skills. I have learned typing, filing, and some data processing, which would be helpful in many new positions since I have had ~~too~~ two years of ~~secreterial~~ secretarial school, I also have learned to be professional, at all times on the job. If I come to work at Ford motor Company, I ~~beleive~~ believe I would do very well at the duties required. When can I come in for an interview?

2. My church group has asked me to write a memo explaining what functions we are planning for this summer.?; I will start off× by saying that all members should have ~~they're~~ their ideas ready by April 1× ~~If~~ they want these ideas to be considered by the group. We will come up with a final list by May 1; ~~It~~ will be approved by the group by May 15. Let's get thinking× ~~So~~ that this summer will be a great one!

7. Using Models

How to Use This Chapter

This chapter provides you with models and exercises for working with a single paragraph. Although these models are intended to help you with your writing, do not think that your paragraphs must look <u>exactly</u> like these. All of the models in this book have the elements of a good paragraph, but they are not the only examples of good writing. When you look at a particular model, try to see what features make it a well-written paragraph. When you do the exercise that follows a model, make sure you include these features in your own piece of writing.

Personal Writing

Letter of Complaint

Dear Sir or Madam:

I am writing to inform you that the fishing gear that I ordered from your company on June 7, 199__, has not arrived yet. My order number is 32890, and I enclose a copy of my canceled check as proof of payment. Because I have been a customer of Slindard's for several years and am usually pleased with your service, I will not cancel my order. However, if this matter is not resolved within the next two weeks, I will have to shop elsewhere for my fishing supplies. Thank you for your help in this matter.

Sincerely,

Bernie Fyre

Exercise A: Writing a Complaint Letter

Perhaps you are not satisfied with the product or service of a company. If so, here is a perfect time to put your complaint in writing. If you do not have such a problem, invent a situation in which you need to write a letter of complaint. Look at the letter on page 132 and take note of the details it includes. Also, refer to the Chapter Checklist for persuasive writing (Chapter 5) for more help in writing this kind of letter. Then write a five- or six-sentence letter of complaint.

Thank-You Letter

Dear Uncle Ralph,

    I really want to thank you for your generous wedding gift of $50. Jonathan and I have decided to use it to buy wallpaper for the bathroom in our new apartment. We chose pale yellow paper with a thin maroon stripe. I know it will look beautiful when it's done. We're looking forward to showing it to you.

Love,

Karin

Exercise B: Writing a Thank-You Letter

Maybe you have someone in mind that you would like to send a thank-you letter to. Remember that you can thank someone for a gift, as in the model above, or for an event you shared, or even for something more personal. The thank-you letter can be written to a close friend or relative (like the one above) or to a more formal acquaintance such as a minister, teacher, or counselor. If you don't have a real situation that calls for a thank-you note, make up an occasion just for practice.

Request to Meet with Child's Teacher

Dear Mr. Angelo:

    I would like to have a meeting with you to discuss my daughter, Wendy Martin. Wendy has never had trouble with English before this year, and I'm concerned about her. She seems to work hard, but her grades remain low. I would like to hear what you have to say about her work. Please call me at my office during the day at 555-9987 or at home during the evening at 555-0912 so we can set a time to meet. Thanks for your time and concern.

Sincerely,

Laura Martin

Exercise C: Writing to Request a Meeting

People have many occasions to request meetings. Sometimes you may want to talk to a teacher, as in the model on page 133. Other times you may need an appointment to see a spiritual leader or perhaps a counselor. Whatever the occasion, you will want to write a letter that is clear and direct.

Letter to the Editor

Dear Editor:

   I am writing to express my serious concern with the way our city's mayor and city council are always arguing. Every day we read new reports about their battles, and every day we see no progress made in the things that really count. While these two groups argue over when their next meeting will be, my family and I worry about whether we will be employed, housed, and fed one more day. When will our government employees stop playing king of the mountain and start doing their jobs?

   Sincerely,

   Ramona Waters

Exercise D: Writing a Letter to the Editor

You may have noticed in your newspaper a section where readers can write in and give their opinions on different issues. These letters are called *letters to the editor*, and they serve as a good place to find out what other people are thinking and feeling as well as a place to express your own point of view.

   Think of something that has been going on in your community that has been bothering you. Or, perhaps something good has happened in your neighborhood that you want other people to know about. Write a letter to the editor expressing your opinion. As in any persuasive paragraph, give your point of view first and support it well.

Application to School

   Educational programs that you apply to might ask you why you want to be in their program. On the following page is a one-paragraph model describing the personal goals that led one student to apply to a night-school program in nursing.

Ever since I started my first job as a cook in a hospital, fifteen years ago, I have been interested in nursing. I always cared a lot about the patients even though I didn't have much contact with them. Now that I have the time to work toward becoming a nurse, I can use my talent and dedication to care for many people. The nursing program at your school has an excellent reputation, and I feel that I am ready for the challenges your program presents.

Exercise E: Writing a School Application

You'll have many forms to fill out when applying to any kind of school program, but one of the most important things you'll write is a description of why you want to go to this school. The model above is an example of some things you might want to include in your paragraph. Even if you're not applying to a school right now, think of a program that might interest you someday. Write a paragraph telling the Admissions Department why you want to be in this program.

Letter for Advice

Dear Abby:

I have a problem that is hard to discuss. I read your column, and I see that you can help other people, so I thought I should try writing to you. I am a twenty-seven-year-old male, and I live with my father. My problem is that he is very protective and is always being nosy about my business. I like to have girlfriends over to the house, but my father is always around, asking questions and annoying us. It is getting embarrassing that a grown man such as myself cannot have some privacy. I have talked to him, but it does no good. I cannot afford to leave home, and besides, my father is ill and needs my help. Abby, what should I do?

Signed,

Sorry Son

Exercise F: Writing to Ask Advice

You may have seen advice columns such as "Dear Abby" in magazines and newspapers. People write in to the column with a question or problem that they need help with. Some of their letters are chosen to be printed and answered. Since no names or addresses are given, a person can feel safe that no one will know his or her problem. Think of a question you would like answered or a problem you want to discuss with an expert. Then write a "Dear Abby" letter.

Business Writing

Job Application Letter

Many times, when looking for a job, you will have to write a short letter to introduce yourself and to ask for an appointment for an interview. For example, you may hear from a friend that a certain company has some openings, and you may want to write to the employment office there.

Dear Sir or Madam:

I am very interested in a position as a data entry clerk with your company. I was referred to you by Ms. Gwen Mugford, who mentioned that you may be hiring at this time. My two years of experience in data entry at Synetrics, Inc., have prepared me well in this field, and I would like a chance to talk with you about your company. Please call me anytime at 555-4141 to set up an appointment. Thank you for your time.

Sincerely,

Chuck Hornstrom

Exercise G: Writing to Apply for a Job

In this exercise, write a letter to apply for a job. Even if you are not interested in applying for a job now, make up a situation and write the letter for practice. Use the model above to help you.

Business Memo

To: Adam Silverton

From: Georgia McKay

Subject: Operation of new weaving equipment

Date: April 7, 199__

Although the new equipment in the weaving room is similar to the old equipment, the employees on my shift do not feel safe operating it without training. We have not been told what to do if it breaks down, and not all of the controls are clearly labeled. Because we are unfamiliar with safety procedures, the current loom speed is dangerously high. We would like you to hold a training session at the beginning of our next shift, which is tomorrow at 4:00.

Exercise H: Writing a Business Memo

People use business memos on the job when something is important enough to be recorded on paper. Many times, questions, directions, and problems get lost, confused, or forgotten if just discussed orally. The memo serves as a short and clear message. In this exercise, use the model on page 136 to help you write a short business memo. If you are not in a situation that calls for memo writing, simply make up a situation in which you need to. This will help your writing improve.

Response to a Warning on the Job

Dear Ms. Royal:

I would like to respond to the letter of warning that I received from you. I understand that my coming late to work many times in the last month has been inconvenient for you and the other salespeople, and I'm sorry. I have been late because my son's school bus route was changed, and now his bus comes later. He is too young to leave by himself. However, I have arranged for him to wait for the bus with a neighbor so I can leave for work earlier. I will be on time every day from now on.

Sincerely,

Leon Garoyan

Exercise I: Writing to Respond to a Warning

Sometimes in the workplace, supervisors feel the need to issue warnings if an employee's work has not been satisfactory. It may be helpful to both employer and employee for the employee to write a response to this warning. In this response, an employee can state whether he or she thinks the warning is fair and what to do about the situation. In this exercise, put yourself in the position of having just received a warning. Write a response, using the model above to guide you.

Job Description

Company: BurgerLover's	**Position:** Quality Leader

Quality leaders are responsible for the quality of food and speed of service received by BurgerLover's customers. With these responsibilities come several tasks. The leader's first duty comes at the beginning of each shift when she assigns each employee to a station. Secondly, it is the job of the quality leader to make sure that all work stations have enough help and that no employees are without work to do. Furthermore, as sales fall off toward the end of a shift, the quality leader assigns employees cleaning jobs. Throughout the shift, the quality leader must watch all work stations to be sure food is prepared according to BurgerLover's standards. Finally, each quality leader fills out a weekly and monthly quality report.

Exercise J: Writing a Job Description

Occasionally on the job you may be asked to write a short description of your duties in a position. Many employers use this as a guide for promotions, raises, reorganizations, etc. As the model above shows, it is important to include the most important of your responsibilities and leave out the less time-consuming ones. Take this opportunity to write a brief but accurate description of your job. If you aren't working, write a description of a position you would like to have and include the important details about the job.

Letter of Resignation

March 1, 199__

Dear Mr. Sahal:

Please accept my resignation as of March 15, 199__. I have accepted an entry-level position with Safer Supermarket. The position is in keeping with my long-term career goals. I have enjoyed working for you, and I have learned a great deal from my experience at Sahal's Furniture Co. Thank you for the opportunity to work with you.

Sincerely,

Connie Monroe

Exercise K: Writing a Letter of Resignation

It is good policy to write a letter of resignation when you leave a job. It is a good record for both you and your employer, and you'll want to be sure you leave with a good reputation. In this exercise, write a letter of resignation using the model above for guidance.

Portfolio Activity #5

Before you begin this final portfolio activity, look through all of your portfolio materials. You should have five paragraphs and all accompanying prewriting materials. Review what you have learned so far by asking yourself these general questions: Do you notice an improvement in your writing ability? What have you learned about your topics? What have you learned about yourself?

Now, rewrite each of your five portfolio assignments into a final form and place the final paragraphs on top of all the materials that correspond to them.

To grade your work, rate your paragraphs on a scale from 1 to 5, with 5 being the highest and 1 the lowest. A paragraph that receives a 5 must be organized, clear, and contain no errors. It must also contain all of the items in your personal checklist. Use the model of a letter to the editor on page 134, and follow these steps.

1. **Ask yourself if the paragraph is organized, clear, and free of errors.** Do you see how the model satisfies these three requirements?

2. **Decide if the paragraph is descriptive, narrative, informative, or persuasive, and refer to the appropriate checklist.** The model is a persuasive paragraph, so look at the checklist for a persuasive paragraph (page 113) to see if the paragraph contains all of the items in the checklist. You will use your personal checklists when you grade your own paragraphs.

3. **Change the statements of the checklist into questions such as the following**: Does the paragraph state an opinion clearly in the topic sentence? Does the paragraph support the opinion with good reasons, accurate facts, or personal experiences? Does the paragraph use transition words between sentences to help the reader understand importance? Does the paragraph end with a strong opinion in the closing sentence? Can the model paragraph answer yes to all of the questions?

Continued

The model paragraph satisfies the first three requirements, and it contains all of the items on the checklist. Therefore, the model receives a final grade of 5.

4. **You will now grade your own paragraphs.** First, for more practice, choose one of the letters you wrote in Chapter 7. Follow the steps in the grading process listed on page 139.

5. Then, **grade all five of your portfolio assignments using the grading process**. It may be helpful for you to take notes as you go through each step. You may also want to write down the questions you create from the checklist statements. On a separate piece of paper, write down what you think your score should be on each paragraph, and turn this sheet in with the rest of your portfolio. Later, compare your findings with those of your instructor.

You have now completed the writing process and this book. Test yourself by seeing if you can remember all of the steps involved in writing a paragraph. If you have correctly followed all of the steps in the writing process, you should now feel more confident in your ability to write. You are now ready to move on to longer pieces of writing. Good luck!